# MYTH AND MODERNITY

SUNY Series, The Margins of Literature
Mihai I. Spariosu, Editor

# MYTH AND MODERNITY

## Postcritical Reflections

MILTON SCARBOROUGH

State University
of New York
Press

Published by
State University of New York Press, Albany

© 1994   State University of New York

Production by Susan Geraghty
Marketing by Terry Swierzowski

Printed in the United States of America

For information, address State University of New York Press,
State University Plaza, Albany, N.Y., 12246

**Library of Congress Cataloging-in-Publication Data**

Scarborough, Milton, 1940–
      Myth and modernity : postcritical reflections / Milton
Scarborough.
            p.   cm. — (SUNY series, the margins of literature)
      Includes bibliographical references and index.
      ISBN 0–7914–1879–0  (alk. paper). — ISBN 0–7914–1880–4 (pbk. :
alk. paper)
      1. Myth. 2. Civilization, Modern—20th century. I. Title.
II. Series.
      BL313.S329   1994
      291.1'3—dc20                                                                 93–17790
                                                                                          CIP

10 9 8 7 6 5 4 3 2 1

*To my mother and father, both teachers*

# CONTENTS

# ACKNOWLEDGMENTS

More than fifteen years of incubation were required for this book to hatch. Its development took place in several stages, each of which relied on the help of many persons. To them all I owe a debt of gratitude.

In the mid-seventies at Centre College I offered a senior-level religion course, "Myths, Models, Metaphors, and the Religious Imagination." A few years later the course was offered under an Integrative Studies rubric as "Myths, Models, Metaphors, and the Human Imagination." In the years since then, numerous groups of Centre students and one group of Emory University students took the course and by their questions and criticisms they helped me give an initial shape to this material.

In the summer of 1978 at Claremont Graduate School my acquaintance with theories of myth was substantially broadened by an NEH Summer Seminar, "Myths, Symbolic Modes, and Ideology," led by Albert B. Friedman.

In the autumn of 1986 I delivered the inaugural Centre lecture, which bore the title "Making Sense of Myth in a World Dominated by Science." Centre's Faculty Development Committee (Carol Bastian, Mike Barton, Walter Nimocks, and Brent White) selected me as the winner of the intramural competition for the lectureship. Ian G. Barbour of Carleton College served as the external referee for that proposal. Centre President Richard Morrill, Dean Leonard DiLillo, and Associate Dean Karin Ciholas provided the funding and a reduction in my teaching duties which made possible the preparation of the lectures, which were my first effort at laying out a general theory of myth.

David Smith, Professor of Religious Studies at Indiana University, read the lectures and gave me an important piece of advice, which I hope to have heeded, namely, to find my own voice.

In March 1987, Ed St. Clair, Chair of the Religion Department at the University of North Carolina at Charlotte, invited me to visit that campus to deliver a general lecture, "The Origin of

Modernity's Hostility to Myth," and to lead a seminar for members of the Religion, Philosophy, and Classics departments on my paper "A Postmodern Understanding of Myth." A year later, at the invitation of Bruce Haddox, Acting Dean, I gave a convocation lecture, "Myth and the Seeing-I Dogma," at Simpson College. These two occasions afforded me the first feedback on the substance of my work on myth by knowledgeable scholars.

In the academic year 1991 to 1992, I enjoyed a year-long sabbatical leave at Emory University, during which the text of the Centre lectures was substantially revised and expanded into the first draft of a book manuscript. I am indebted to Centre President Michael Adams and Dean John Ward for their approval and partial funding of that sabbatical leave. Also, The Southeastern Humanities Consortium and Emory University, with the help of a grant from the Dana Corporation, underwrote the remainder of my sabbatical expenses. In addition, Emory University provided me with housing, office space, library privileges, and a top priority parking sticker for the year.

A number of people read the rough draft of the book and made helpful suggestions. They include the other Dana Fellows for 1991 to 1992 (Derek Barkalow of Stetson University, Gil Johnston of Eckerd College, Bill Pickens of Morehouse College, Valarie Ziegler of Rhodes College), Emory graduate student and Dana seminar participant Gilbert Bond, Robert Detweiler of Emory University, and William H. Poteat of Duke University. Valarie Ziegler insisted that I break up long, Germanic paragraphs into more manageable chunks. Several written exchanges and several long lunches with Bob Detweiler, Professor of Comparative Literature at Emory and Director of the Dana Fellows Program, were especially significant for the final shape of the book.

Thanks to Centre's Faculty Development Committee (Carol Bastian, Steve Froehlich, Mykol Hamilton, Bruce Johnson, Tom McCollough, and Phyllis Passeriello), I received a faculty development grant for the summer of 1992, which enabled me to make revisions in the manuscript prior to sending it out to publishers. William H. Poteat of Duke and William Weston of Centre read the revised manuscript, as did Bill Rogers of Furman University, who made numerous recommendations that I have incorporated into the text.

Among those persons making bibliographical suggestions were Bob Detweiler of Emory University, Bill Rogers and Edgar

McKnight of Furman University, Mark Rasmussen of Centre, and Steve Wolfgang of Danville, Kentucky.

When two wordprocessing softwares failed to speak to each other in a civil manner, Patsy McAfee retyped many of the text's footnotes. Judy Bowell strayed far beyond the boundaries of her job description to make copies of the manuscript.

The University of California Press gave me permission to use the poem "These Days" by Charles Olson from page 106 of its 1987 publication *The Collected Poetry of Charles Olson*, translated and edited by George Butterick.

Finally, I wish to thank my editors from SUNY Press, Carola Sautter and Susan Geraghty, for smoothing the path toward publication. Special thanks are due to Rebecca Hogancamp, my copy-editor, whose eye for stylistic errors is like that of an eagle: to Erin Roberts, my student assistant, who endured the tedium of proofreading the galley and page proofs; and to Mike Hamm, my division chair, for providing funds to cover miscellaneous expenses required for the preparation of the manuscript.

The reader will, I trust, absolve all the persons named above from any of the book's limitations.

# CHAPTER 1

# *Modernity and the Crisis of Myth*

In July of 1969, a dugout canoe carrying anthropologist Edmund Carpenter and his crew headed for a spot on the bank of the Sepik River where a solitary figure stood awaiting their arrival. The figure was the chief of a Stone Age tribe living in a remote area of New Guinea. The Australian administrators of Papua and New Guinea had hired Carpenter to recommend effective ways of communicating with the native peoples who were under their supervision. As Carpenter stepped ashore, the other villagers were nowhere to be seen, but when gifts were given to the chief, the natives began peeking out from their places of concealment and slowly coming forward. The distribution of balloons and other gifts soon won Carpenter the trust of the villagers and permission to conduct a series of experiments among them.

The experiments involved the use of assorted items of modern technology. Each villager was given a small mirror and a Polaroid portrait of himself or herself. Only when Carpenter and his helpers pointed to features of the images and then to the corresponding features of their faces did the villagers understand the images. Next, the voices of the villagers were recorded and played back to them. As these experiments were conducted, motion pictures were made of the natives' reactions and, once developed, were shown to the villagers.

Upon hearing their voices coming from a metal box, the natives jumped back, began shouting in anger and fright and brandishing their spears. The reactions to the visual experiments were similar to each other and different from the auditory one.

They seemed paralyzed by the sight of their own images. Rooted to the spot, they stared at the mirrors, transfixed, their stomach muscles trembling in tension. Suddenly having become acutely self-conscious, they would slip away from each other and in solitude gaze intently at their portraits. In a very short time,

however, the fear of the gadgets vanished and villagers were play-
fully making photos of each other and wearing them on their fore-
heads.

At the conclusion of the experiments, Carpenter left to analyze his data. When he returned to the village in December 1969,
just six months after his initial arrival, he was shocked at what he
found. He reported:

> At first I thought I had made a mistake and come to the wrong
> place. It had changed completely. Houses had been rebuilt in a
> new style. The men wore European clothes, carried themselves
> differently, acted differently. They had left the village after our
> visit and, for the first time, travelled outside the world they had
> previously known. . . . Suddenly the cohesive village had become
> a collection of separate, private individuals. Like the hero of
> Matthew Arnold's poem, they wandered "between two worlds,
> one dead, the other powerless to be born."[1]

Subsequently, Carpenter reports, the most sacred ceremony of the
tribe, the male initiation rite, was made voluntary and permission
to film the disclosure of the sacred mysteries was given to the out-
siders. Despite the fact that previously no woman had ever been
allowed near the disclosure, a woman was admitted to operate
one of the cameras. Religious leaders even halted the ritual temporarily to give her time to insert fresh film. It was announced,
moreover, that this would be the last involuntary male initiation
and that the sacred water drums, the most important objects in
the ritual, were being put up for sale.

What are we to make of this incident? It is not necessary to
idealize the New Guineans to appreciate the magnitude of what
befell them. Remember, theirs was a Stone Age culture. Not only
had they never encountered Europeans before, but they had never
even become acquainted with neighboring tribes. When hunters of
two villages caught sight of each other in the forest, both fled in
terror. Beyond that, not simply a ritual but also the myth intimately associated with it and, indeed, the way of life which sustained the myth and ritual and was, in turn, sustained by them
were dealt a life-threatening blow. Perhaps it would not be too
strong to speak of the event as a cultural murder. To use the term
murder, however, is almost inevitably, at least for those of us who
read mystery novels, to raise the standard questions: Who did it?
By what means? What was the motive?

Carpenter himself is quick to take the blame and acknowledges that his actions may have been immoral. He says:

> . . . I am convinced (and horrified) that this was a direct result of our experiment. Our actions had produced instant alienation. They had destroyed the natives' old, strictly tribal self-concept.
>
> In one brutal movement, these villagers had been hoisted out of a Stone Age existence and transformed from tribesmen into detached individuals, lonely, frustrated, alienated. They were no longer at home in their old environment or, for that matter, anywhere.[2]

He identifies the electronic media as the means of this cultural upheaval and expresses concern for the effect the media may be having on us. As for motive, the outcome was wholly unintended.

This assessment, however, appears to me to be too simple. First of all, although there existed at that time no anthropology of tourism, a recent subspecialty treating the ways in which tourists affect and are affected by their visits to more traditional societies, surely it has been known since the onset of anthropological field work that the study of oral societies inadvertently triggers significant changes in them, not all of which are beneficial. If that is true for the relatively passive participant observer approach, it might easily have been suspected that the more aggressive approach taken by Carpenter would likely amplify the usual effects. Second, Carpenter need not shoulder all the blame. He was an agent of the Australian administrators of the region, although probably in a better position than they to predict the outcome of his visit to the village. Finally, it is not altogether clear that the electronic equipment was the means of the cultural death. In "The Writing Lesson," a chapter of his *Triste Tropiques*, Claude Lévi-Strauss, whose encounter with the Amerindian Nambik-wara destroyed their previously alleged idyllic existence, points the finger at writing. Having seen him take notes in front of them, they very quickly grasped the ways in which this foreign technique could be used to gain an advantage for themselves over other members of the tribe.[3] In the light of Lévi-Strauss's analysis it seems to me more likely that the social changes were effected by neither writing nor the electronic media per se but by both of these technologies as embodiments of some larger cultural force. Indeed, on this reading, all the actions of Carpenter, his assistants, and the government officials—not just the technologies—would manifest the same cultural force and, therefore, contribute to the tribal crisis.

The New Guinea story becomes, then, not simply the tale about what happened to a few hundred natives on a remote island in the Pacific Ocean. It can be read as an allegory about Western civilization. Just as in time-lapse photography the events that take place over an extended period are telescoped into a few minutes or seconds, so what has happened in the West imperceptibly slowly over the centuries was repeated in this New Guinea village in a matter of months, bringing the longer trend into focus.

At least since the nineteenth century the West has been conscious of the death of its myths. In the twentieth century it has become common among intellectuals to speak of the crisis of myth. For some, of course, the death of myth is no crisis at all but a liberation from superstitious beliefs and unnecessary restrictions. For others, however—among them religious persons and poets—there has been a lamentable crisis. Philip Wheelwright described the situation as follows:

> This loss of myth-consciousness I believe to be the most devastating loss that humanity can suffer; for as I have argued, myth-consciousness is the bond that unites men both with one another and with the unplumbed Mystery from which mankind is sprung and without reference to which the radical significance of things goes to pot. Now a world bereft of radical significance is not long tolerated; it leaves men radically unstable, so that they will seize at any myth or pseudomyth that is offered.[4]

The death of myth, however, is not a peculiarly modern phenomenon. The appearance in classical Greece of theories about the nature and function of myths already indicates that myths had become problematic in some sense, that naive reliance on them was no longer possible. The purpose of those theories was somehow to heal the existential wound made by being cut off from a simple, direct participation in a mythological world. According to Richard Chase, the theories of myth arising from the classical world were three in number.[5]

The euhemerist theory, named for a Messenian of the fourth century B.C.E., claims that the gods of myths are actually human conquerors, rulers, or philosophers whose oral biographies were embellished and distorted almost beyond recognition at the hands of imaginative storytellers. Euhemerus arrived at this view as a result of visiting an island off the coast of Arabia. There he found a temple, one of whose columns bore an inscription which said that Zeus was a man who was born and died on Crete and who was later deified by an admiring populace. On this view, myths are vastly inflated human history. Chase notes that this theory became a weapon in the hands of some fathers of the Christian church to discredit pagan myths. It was also used by Boccaccio in the Renaissance, Diderot and Hume in the eighteenth century, and Herbert Spencer in the nineteenth century. It continues to have some currency.

2 The Christian-apologetic theory has, according to Chase, two varieties. One of them, Plagiarism, also used by early church fathers and by some minor figures in the seventeenth century, holds that anything of value to be found in pagan myths was borrowed illicitly from Judaism. Greek gods were taken from the Old Testament and then corrupted. Condescension, on the other hand, admits to some paganlike crudities in Judaism but says that God permitted their inclusion as a necessary, intermediate step toward a higher revelation. The church fathers, of course, not to mention the laity, were unwilling to use the term myth of Christian stories.

3 In Chase's view, the most important theory emanating from the ancient world regarded myths as allegories. In a few cases myths were said to be about metaphysical concepts; in others they were seen as didactic moral allegories. By and large, however, the Ionians, Stoics, medieval poets, and Renaissance humanists understood myths to be allegories of nature in which each deity represented some aspect of the natural order. The Stoics, for example, understood Hera to be air, Hades to be vapor, Hephaestus to be fire, and Demeter to be earth. The story of Hephaestus' expulsion from heaven is actually a description of primitive people obtaining fire from flashes of lightning.

The crisis which generated these theories of myth involved particular, pagan myths. The impact of these theories on the viability of myth itself was limited. Christendom was interested in history understood as the drama of God's redemption of His creation; it was not interested in nature. Hence it used euhemerism and plagiarism to counter pagan polytheism, morals, anthropology, and history while, at the same time, never acknowledging its own stories as myths. As for the allegories of nature, few thinkers prior to the modern era seriously questioned their validity. Allegory, after all, implies the self-conscious encoding in a one-to-one correspondence elements of one universe of discourse in that of another. Thus, descriptions of features or events of nature were believed to be encoded in personifications characterized as divinities. This meant that such clever, sophisticated stories, when properly decoded, could be seen to square with observations made by scientist and nonscientist alike. Properly understood, then, even pagan nature myths could be regarded as true.

The dying of myths, however, antedates even classical Greece and is by no means limited to the West. Very probably it has been a persistent feature of all human history and prehistory. In endless succession Anu gave way to Marduk, Dyaus was banished by Indra, and the Maori god Rangi was replaced by Tangaroa. Whether by conquest, social upheaval, or intercultural contact, myths rise, have their day, then perish. From this perspective the New Guinea tale is but another chapter in the eternal human drama, and if it is an allegory, it is an allegory about that perennial drama.

If Carpenter's story is read in this last way, however, its true significance will go undetected. It was Sherlock Holmes who taught us that the scene of the crime often conceals clues that can unravel a case. The principal clue at the New Guinea village is that the traditional myth, unlike the perennial drama described above, has not been replaced by a new one. No new initiation rite has been constructed. No new mysteries have been discovered or hidden inside the sacred enclosure or revealed to those young males who are duly prepared. Nor has the old complex of myths and rituals disappeared entirely. There is only an attenuated clinging to the devitalized traditional myth and ritual. Myth is not so much dead as it is broken, enervated, numbed.   sapped of energy

This numbing and the absence of the renewal of myth are the calling card of modernity. As late as the mid-sixteenth century, near the dawn of the modern age, when the Spanish missionaries, soldiers, and civilians came to "New Spain" to missionize and exploit the native American peoples, the effect was different from New Guinea. Under the tolerant Jesuits the religion of the Pima and Papago of Arizona incorporated elements of Catholic Christianity and remained vital. Even when the rigid Franciscans confiscated the paraphanalia and forbade the ceremonials of the Pueblo peoples, the religion simply went underground and remained strong.[6] By contrast, there is something in the touch of modernity which destroys not simply some particular myth but also myth itself. Modernity seems to result in the termination of the possibility of having any vital myth whatsoever. Indeed, modernity is that era in our history in which the elimination of myth itself became for some a self-conscious goal. Modernity, then, not Western civilization generally or some universal and perennial process, will be our prime suspect in the crime at the New Guinea village.

A change in suspect, of course, prompts a reconsideration of both motive and means. The question of means will be the focus of considerable attention in the course of this work and will be the occasion for examining the nature of myth and modernity. In the chapter that immediately follows this one, however, we will seek to discover what there is about modernity, the probable culprit in a cultural murder, that is so inimical to myth. We shall discover that the theories of myth put forward by modernity reflect an epistemological and/or ontological commitment to dualism, with the result that myth is understood in either a reductionistic or fragmented way. Chapter 3 examines some of the few theories which acknowledge that myth exists within modernity. We learn, however, that they either redefine myth so as to make it unrecognizable and trivial or reserve some part of modernity which is held to be myth-free. Chapter 4 will demonstrate that no part of modernity escapes an ongoing grounding in myth. In particular, it investigates the ways in which the Timaeus and Genesis tacitly inform some of our most sophisticated scientific, philosophical, and logical theories. Chapter 5 points out some of the ways in which twentieth-century physics undermines the scientific basis for the rise of modernity. It also sets forth a new definition of myth which is heavily indebted to Maurice Merleau-Ponty's existential-phenomenological understanding of the the life-world and the body-subject. Chapter 6 treats the question of the truth of myth, including the myths which inform this volume. In addition, it portrays modernity as committed, on the level of imagination, to a visualist model of knowing. Finally, the story of Abraham's departure from Ur of the Chaldees for the Promised Land is read as an epistemological allegory of special relevance for our movement into a postmodern world.

epistemological
, ontological
reductionist
dualism – 2 forms of reality
, dichotomy – 2 parts

# CHAPTER 2

# Modernity on Myth

... The more we are entranced by the dance of matter the more
we fall victim to its fissive nature. It's not only the atom that splits.
We are in its mirror. Consciousness splits too. It shatters like china.
—Lindsay Clarke, *The Chymical Wedding*

At the end of Chapter 1 modernity became our chief suspect in the
crime against the New Guinea peoples. Insofar as that event is an
allegory of what has happened imperceptibly in the West over the
past several centuries, modernity is also implicated in the larger
crisis of myth. Modernity, in other words, may be a serial killer.
What is modernity? What is its modus operandi?

The division of the history of the West into three ages—
ancient, middle, and modern—was the invention of modernists
themselves. They were motivated by the desire to make a radically
new beginning in history. Such an absolute beginning required
that the past be absolutely eradicated. Currently, thinkers herald-
ing the arrival of postmodernity are engaged in enumerating the
specific features of the modern worldview.

In the natural sciences one might argue that modernity began
with Copernicus or Kepler, but there might be more agreement on
Galileo. The sciences reserve the term modern for twentieth-century or even more recent discoveries and use "classical" for the
revolution of the seventeenth century. In philosophy, the modern
era is often tied to Descartes' turn to the subjective realm and to
the rise of epistemology. Postmodernists see modernity's fullest
expression and, perhaps, the beginning of its termination in the
philosophy of Hegel. Whatever the niceties of precise dating or
characterization might be, what concerns us is a clue to its hostility to myth. In this chapter that clue is said to be the ontological
dualism prefigured in the distinction, made by Kepler and Galileo,
between primary and secondary qualities and elaborated into a
systematic philosophy by Descartes. We will discover that modern
theories interpret myths as referring, when properly understood,

to some aspect of mind (the inside) or, in a primitive and mistaken fashion, to some feature of the objective world (the outside). This dualism of inner and outer will form the basis for a scheme for the classification of modern myth theories. Determined solely by ontological reference, the scheme will be augmented by the categories "up," "middle," and "down" in view of the fact that the ontological dimensions of the various disciplines are often arranged, like the Great Chain of Being, in a hierarchy extending from matter to spirit. The vertical categories of the inside are not necessarily correlates of the vertical categories of the outside. So interpreted, the meaning of myth in modernity is restricted to a fragment of one half of this dualism and, moreover, is reduced to what is expressible in the terms of an abstract, disciplinary methodology. By and large, the result is that myth becomes associated with the primitive, the past, the subjective, and the untrue.

## THE NATURE OF MODERNITY

In her *Philosophy in a New Key* Susanne Langer suggests that if there are philosophical epochs, they are defined in terms of a fundamental question to which the various persons or schools of the period offer their often divergent answers. Thales, for example, asked about the identity of the basic stuff from which all things were made. This question defined the pre-Socratic epoch, during which, along with Thales himself, such philosopher-scientists as Anaxagoras, Anaximander, Anaximanes, Empedocles, and Democritus proposed as answers, in turn, water, earth, the boundless, fire, all of the above in different proportions, and atoms. The Socratic epoch began, says Langer, when Socrates posed another fundamental question: For what goal in life ought people to strive? While there was general agreement that the correct answer was happiness, the subsequent debate concerned whether the cause of happiness was wealth, fame, power, or care for one's soul. As for the modern epoch, Langer writes:

> This new epoch had a mighty and revolutionary generative idea: the dichotomy of all reality into inner experience and outer world, subject and object, private reality and public truth.[1]

The bifurcation of reality into inner experience and outer world received its definitive philosophical expression in the work of

Descartes, but the crucial moves were made earlier by Copernicus, Kepler, and Galileo, who in the course of founding modern science created a new metaphysics of the natural world.

In his *The Metaphysical Foundations of Modern Science* E. A. Burtt stresses the central role of mathematics in this intellectual revolution. For Aristotle, quantity, and thus mathematics, was only one of ten fundamental categories in terms of which reality was to be described and explained; the highest priority was given to logic. The founding by the Medicis in Florence of a new academy prompted a revival of Plato's thought, which spread across southern Europe in the fifteenth and sixteenth centuries and posed a challenge to the Aristotelianism which had been dominant since the thirteenth century. *Timaeus,* the work upon which this revival of Platonism was so heavily dependent, emphasizes the mathematical religion of Pythagoras. Wherever this neo-Pythagorean revival spread, math replaced logic as the most fundamental discipline.

Copernicus and Kepler were ardent Pythagoreans and shared with Galileo the belief that the universe was made of numbers. To know what was true of nature one had only to discover what was true of mathematics. These metaphysical convictions rested almost entirely on the aesthetics of simplicity and harmony and, in the case of Kepler, a superstitious involvement in sun worship. Hence, for Copernicus and Kepler, whose gaze was directed at the heavens, nature became that which can be stated in mathematical laws describing in the simplest terms the observed motions of the planets.

For Galileo, who lowered his gaze to include the terrestrial realm, where objects can be manipulated as well as observed, nature was what can be stated in mathematical laws describing the relations of variables measured in experimental situations. It follows that nature consists of lengths, widths, shapes, positions, directions, velocities, and accelerations—that is, those features which are measurable and expressible in the language of math.

Kepler was the first to distinguish these "primary qualities" from such "secondary qualities" as taste, touch, sound, smell, and the nonmeasurable visual qualities, such as color. Galileo adopted Kepler's distinction but added the notion that only primary qualities are real; secondary qualities were not actually in things but were in the mind only. Secondary qualities were not permanent, they varied from person to person, they were not measurable, and they were not expressible in the language of math. Here, then, begins the dichotomy into inner and outer. Burtt concludes:

Now, in the course of translating this distinction of primary and secondary into terms suited to the new mathematical interpretation of nature, we have the first stage in the reading of man quite out of the real and primary realm. . . . His performances could not be treated by the quantitative method, except in the most meager fashion. His was a life of colours and sounds, of pleasures, of griefs, of passionate loves, of ambitions, and strivings. Hence the real world must be the world outside man.[2]

It was this view to which Descartes gave a systematic philosophical expression. The outside world was "extended substance." This included human bodies understood as machines. Since knowledge requires the existence of mind as knower, Descartes added a second kind of reality, "thinking substance." This includes the mind of God and human minds. Mind and its experience constitutes the inner realm. For Descartes, "all human science consists *simply* in distinguishing these notions, and in attributing each of them only to those things to which they pertain (emphasis mine)."[3] He saw this distinction as the key to the possibility of achieving absolutely certain knowledge. It provided modernity with its agenda. The failure of previous ages consisted precisely in their failure to apply this distinction. Early modern thinkers believed that when all things were properly sorted out into one or the other of these two bins, all error and superstition would disappear and human history would become fully rational.


## MODERNITY AND MYTH

The division of all reality into inner experience and outer world had implications for myth that were clear and devastating. Myth must be about one or the other. The ancient and medieval view of myths as allegories of nature would no longer work. Not even in some esoteric allegorical code can myths be about lengths, widths, shapes, positions, directions, and locomotions. If myths are about nature, then they must be about a nature comprised of secondary qualities. Such a nature, however, exists only in the human mind as a figment of the imagination; it is unreal. The result is that myths understood as allegories of nature could no longer be squared with science. The cosmological function of myth, the telling of the story of the whole of the universe, was discredited. The inner-outer program also required a distinction between myth and history. History was about events which happened in the objective world; consequently, myth was an additional and fictional layer of meaning superimposed on top of the objective world by the irrational or prerational mind.

It was the Enlightenment, the era in which modernity came to dominance, that drew out most relentlessly the implications of the inner-outer dichotomy for myth. They were entirely negative. In this period myth became what it remains today in the popular imagination—namely, a cipher for all that is false. For Fontenelle, myths were "only a mass of chimeras, dreams, and absurdities."[4] Pierre Bayle regarded myth as a falsehood believed by persons with weak minds. Voltaire asserted that myths were invented by scheming priests or politicians for the purpose of oppressing or controlling the populace. For Diderot and D'Alembert they were absurd, degrading, and impossible to analyze.

The negative conclusions of the Englightenment did not, however, succeed in eliminating academic interest in myth. Scholars of the nineteenth and twentieth centuries, while agreeing with the Enlightenment that myth was false, held that it was both analyzable and meaningful. Their ways of rehabilitating myth vary widely in disciplinary affiliation and methodology, but all share a strategy characteristic also of pre-Englightenment views. It consists of saying that although myths appear at a superficial level to be about gods, goddesses, tricksters, monsters, etc., in fact they are about something else. Mythic language, then, is not literal but in some sense symbolic.

The something else to which scholars said the myths actually refer is an indication of the ontology always implied by any disciplinary methodology and the clue to what distinguishes all modern theories from ancient and medieval ones as well as from postcritical ones. If Langer is correct, as I believe she is, in pointing to the inner-outer dichotomy as the defining mark of modernity, then all myth theories insofar as they are modern will also reflect that dichotomy. The dichotomy may appear in the original ontological form or its derivative epistemological form and, more than likely, it will appear indirectly rather than directly.

What I intend to do is to devise a classification system which exhibits the ontological orientation of modern myth theories. The principal categories of the system will be "inside" and "outside." The system will be further differentiated and refined by the addition of "up," "middle," and "down." These secondary categories relate to an ontological hierarchy which appears in different and not necessarily correlated forms in both the outside and inside realms. Each category in the system will be defined by two terms, one principal and one secondary. The result is a classification system of six categories: outside down, outside middle, outside up, inside up, inside middle, inside down. The system is visually displayed in the form of a chart, which appears at the end of this chapter (Table 1). Although the chart contains additional, incidental information, its categories and the location of theories within them are determined exclusively by the ontological referent of "myth" stated in or implied by the various myth theories themselves.

In what follows it is not my intention to provide a comprehensive survey of modern myth theories but to treat enough theories to illustrate the classification system.[5] The theories treated are ones with which I have become familiar in teaching an undergraduate course on myth for over a decade; in that sense the selection is somewhat arbitrary.

## Outside Down

Outside down theories agree with all modern theories that myths are analyzable, meaningful, nonliteral, and false. They are distinguished, however, by additional common features. First, myth is the product of so-called primitive societies, some of which have survived into the modern age. Second, all of them hold that myth is really about nature. Because of the work of science, modernity understands that nature is an objective reality lying outside the mind and is properly described by empirically verifiable mathematical procedures. It is precisely the failure of "primitive" peoples to distinguish the inside from the outside that renders their mythologies false. Third, myth is a primitive form of philosophy or science in that it springs from a merely theoretical interest in describing and explaining the natural order. Because nature is comprised of matter, I have termed these theories "down" in accordance with the Chains of Being and other hierarchical schemes familiar in the West.

**Max Mueller: Myth as Explanation for Aryan Metaphors.**  It was the theorists of the nineteenth century and the first decade of this century for whom nature was the almost exclusive answer to the question as to what myth is really about. For the most part, these theorists were either German philologists or English comparative anthropologists. The best known of the philologists was Max Mueller(1823–1900), who, although German, lived for most of his career in England. For him, myths were the result of a cultural degeneration which occurred when the strong and noble Aryan peoples, uncorrupted by the artificial restraints of civilization, migrated from their homeland to Europe. In the steppes of Russia they spoke the Aryan language, whose peculiarity lay in containing nothing but metaphors. In such a language communication takes place by the processes of polyonymy, in which one word has several meanings ("Dyaus" can mean "sun," "dawn," "light"), and homonymy, in which several words have the same meaning (usually "sun"). As a consequence, metaphor arises when several nouns ("sun," "brightness") are created from a single verb ("to shine") and when the several nouns are transferred to a single object (the sun). People wishing simply to remark that the sun had come up were forced to utter "Night gives birth to a brilliant child." Such a language, says Mueller, is "diseased" because, lacking the resources by which people can give full expression to their emotions, it produces a special kind of insanity.

When the Aryans moved into Greece, they retained the metaphors of their language but forgot the original meanings. The Greeks, puzzled, for example, by "Endymion" (an Aryan metaphor for "sunset") and "Selene" (an Aryan metaphor for "moon"), created a story about a young man climbing a mountain, falling asleep, and being found and loved by a maid. Thus, a myth was born. An Aryan, by contrast, merely used the terms to say that the sun had set and the moon risen.[6] Myths can be explained, according to Mueller, when the Aryan language is reconstructed by isolating the common elements in its derivatives (Greek, Latin, Celtic, Sanskrit, etc.) and the mythic elements traced back to their original Aryan metaphors. When this is done, Mueller said, it will be seen that most of the myths are about features of the heavens, primarily the sun.

**The English Anthropologists: Myth as Animism, Totemism, and Magic.**    For Mueller myth was the product of a culture which had degenerated to a more primitive level. For the English anthropologists, under the influence of Darwin, myth is the product of cultures which have not yet evolved to a higher level. It is not the result of diseased language but actual, prelinguistic experience of nature understood as animistic, magical, and totemistic.

For E. B. Tylor (1832–1917), all myth is explicable in terms of animism alone. Animism, which understands the various objects of nature, especially those which move, as inhabited by souls or other spirits, marks the beginnings of a cultural evolution which moves through universal, fixed stages. Human souls are posited to account for images seen in dreams and other mental phenomena or reflected in water. Souls are projected into nature because of analogies between aspects of nature and human beings. The swaying limbs of a tree are like humans moving their arms, legs, or trunks. As at least semiautonomous beings, the souls and spirits can interact with humans and affect their well-being; consequently, it is important to make offerings to or otherwise placate them.

Andrew Lang (1844–1912) and Sir James Frazer (1854–1941) took up Tylor's animism but added both magic and totemism as explanatory theories. To Frazer, culture develops from magic through religion to science. Like science, of which it is a primitive and illusory form, magic operates according to laws. The Law of Similarity states that imitating a desired effect will cause it to occur. A fish in a bowl of water placed by the riverbank will cause fish to appear in the river at that point, to the delight and profit of fishermen. The Law of Contagion or contact states that if X (a hair or a fingernail, for example) was once in contact with Y (John Doe), then whatever is done to X will happen also to Y.

The force operating in magic was conceived gradually by incorporating "preanimism" into "*mana*." Robert R. Marett (1866–1943) proposed a magico-religious stage more primitive than Tylor's animism. This "preanimism" or "animatism" attributed life and personality to aspects of nature without positing a distinct soul. The tree itself, not its inhabitant, is a spirit. Mana, first identified by Robert Henry Codrington (1830–1922), is an eerie, impersonal, dangerous force present in rituals, spells, fetishes (objects), and special persons. Tabus are the procedures which must be followed to handle mana with impunity. Mana is understood to obey Frazer's laws.

A third device, employed by Lang and Frazer, was totemism. The concept was also adopted and adapted by van Gennep, Freud, and Durkheim. Perhaps the strongest of its diverse forms is that a human social group (a clan, for example) is believed to be related by blood or a shared substance to an animal or plant group or a natural object. The humans are obligated to protect the totem.

Annually, the humans eat the plant or animal in a special ritual, presumably to receive its powers. In some versions of the theory, the totems have the power to turn into their human relatives, and at death humans turn into their totems. Totem animals are sometimes said to fight alongside their human counterparts in battles against their enemies.

## Outside Middle

**Bronislaw Malinowski: Myth as Social Charter.**   While his predecessors sat in armchairs in Germany or England, comparing texts or stories, Bronislaw Malinowski (1884–1942) went to the Trobriand Islands to do fieldwork. That fact resulted in several significant departures from the work of the earlier scholars.

First, methods more like those of the natural sciences were required. Thus, he examined maps and village censuses, used statistical documentation, and constructed tables. Even when his methods were not mathematical, they were empirical. He examined schedules of people's workday; collected native interpretations of their own folklore, customs, and rituals; and observed the tone of voice in conversations around the campfire.

Second, Malinowski argued that myth is not primitive philosophy or science, not the detached speculations of the intellect, not knowledge for knowledge's sake; rather, it serves basic, everyday needs in the life of a people. This functionalist approach is summed up in a now-famous quote:

> Studied alive, myth, as we shall see, is not symbolic, but a direct expression of its subject matter; it is not an explanation in satisfaction of a scientific interest, but a narrative resurrection of a primeval reality, told in satisfaction of deep religious wants, moral cravings, social submissions, even practical requirements. Myth fulfills in primitive culture an indispensable function: it expresses, enhances, and codifies belief; it safeguards and enforces morality; it vouches for the efficiency of ritual and contains practical rules for the guidance of man. Myth is thus a vital ingredient of human civilization; it is not an idle tale, but a hardworked active force; it is not an intellectual explanation or an artistic imagery, but a pragmatic charter of primitive faith and moral wisdom.[7]

Third, he noted that the Trobriand Islanders classified their traditional stories as *kukwanebu* (untrue stories owned by individuals and told in dramatic performances for amusement at special seasons), *libwongo* (allegedly true stories about the achievements of heroes, told without drama by their relatives at any time), or *liliu* (sacred, true stories justifying social arrangements, morality, and rituals) and that this system makes clear that myths are not always about history or nature.

Finally, like Frazer, Mueller, etc., Malinowski understands myth to be about an outside. This should be obvious from his methodology. He does use "Psychology" in the title of his most considered work on myth, but he learned his psychology from Wilhelm Wundt and Karl Buehler. The true object of myth for Malinowski, however, is not nature but society. Both totemism and magic, of course, involve a relation to plants, animals, or other aspects of nature, but Malinowski emphasizes their function in society. To discern the full meaning of myth, he says, "we are gradually led to build up the full theory of native social organization."

### Outside Up

As society partially transcends nature, so the spiritual transcends both. In this category myths are understood not simply to appear to be but actually to be about the gods and goddesses which move through the story lines. The gods are objectively real and the myths, although not necessarily literally so, are true. That such views might be found among thinkers of a theologically conservative bent is predictable enough; that these conservatives might be willing to call the stories in which they believe "myths" is surprising. Just such is the case, however, for Clark Pinnock, J. R. R. Tolkien, and John Warwick Montgomery. C. S. Lewis, the best known of these theorists, will serve as our example.

**C.S. Lewis: Myth as Fable and Fact.**    Borrowing a page from Aristotle's *Poetics*, Lewis sees myth as having a special logic which solves a human dilemma. The dilemma is that all our experiences are concrete; they are of this flower, this pungent odor. Thought, by contrast, is abstract and universal. We can stand outside the experience of ice cream and know its general properties, in which case "fudge ripple" becomes a mere example of a universal type. On the other hand, we can taste a cold, sweet mouthful of the substance. Unfortunately, eating yields nothing we would wish to call knowledge. Myth, however, provides a mediating option. It does contain a universal truth, expressible in abstract terms, but it does so in as near a concrete form as is possible for us. The concreteness of myth permits us to experience the reality which is the myth's referent. Lewis puts it this way:

> What flows into you from the myth is not truth but reality (truth is always *about* something, but reality is that *about which* truth is), and, therefore, every myth becomes the father of innumerable truths on the abstract level. . . . It is not, like truth, abstract; nor is it, like direct experience, bound to the particular.[8]

Myths are stories, to be sure, says Lewis, but they are those stories which possess "extra-literary" characteristics. They are about the impossible and preternatural, they do not prompt the reader to identify with their characters, they are grave, they inspire awe and numinous feelings, and they make little use of narrative features such as suspense and surprise. This definition, given largely in terms of the reader's response, implies that what will count as myth will vary from person to person.[9]

The greatest of all myths—what is elsewhere called "The Grand Miracle"—is the Incarnation of God in Jesus Christ. That God, out of love, descended to earth to live, die, and rise again in order to save human beings from sin and eternal damnation is, indeed, a fable, but it is unique in that it came true.

> Now as myth transcends thought, Incarnation transcends myth. The heart of Christianity is a myth which is also a fact. The old myth of the Dying God, *without ceasing to be myth*, comes down from the heaven of legend and imagination to the earth of history. It *happens*—at a particular date, in a particular place, followed by definable historical consequences. We pass from a Balder or an Osiris, dying nobody knows when or where, to a historical Person crucified (it is all in order) *under Pontius Pilate*. By becoming fact it does not cease to be myth; that is the miracle.[10]

The stories of dying and rising vegetation gods, found everywhere in the world, were not plagiarized from Christianity but, in what might be understood as a modern twist on the condescension theory, are anticipations of Christ. Lewis can say:

> God is more than a god, not less; Christ is more than Balder, not less. We must not be ashamed of the mythical radiance resting on our theology. We must not be nervous about 'parallels' and 'Pagan Christs': they *ought* to be there—it would be a stumbling block if they weren't.[11]

Thus, a general theory of myth is put at the service of Christian theology. This is not a matter of subjective decision or mere fideism. For Lewis, the reality of what he claims is guaranteed by an objective reason, which invades the human body from the outside the way God invaded His creation in the Incarnation.

## Inside Up

Few people doubt the existence of nature and society; the latter lie open before our senses. Traditionally, even the imperceptible spiritual realm has been taken for granted as real. By contrast, claims for the existence of an inside are of more recent origin, and the mapping of its terrain has been largely a phenomenon of this century. Theorists of the inside are, consequently, much more likely than those of the outside to mention the inner-outer dichotomy in the course of carving out and seeking to establish a region in which the mechanisms they postulate can be said to operate.

**Ernst Cassirer: Myth as an Organ of Self-Revelation.**    For neo-Kantian Ernst Cassirer (1874–1945), the skepticism which has reduced myth to a mere fiction is the result of the futile effort to understand it in terms of an outside. At the outset of his *Language and Myth*, he makes the shift inward:

> Against this self-dissolution of the spirit there is only one remedy: to accept in all seriousness what Kant calls his "Copernican revolution." Instead of measuring the content, meaning, and truth of intellectual forms by something extraneous which is supposed to be reproduced in them, we must find in these forms themselves the measure and criterion for their truth and intrinsic meaning. Instead of taking them as mere copies of something else, we must see in each of these spiritual forms a spontaneous law of generation; an original way and tendency of expression which is more than a mere record of something initially given in fixed categories of real existence. From this point of view, myth, art, language, and science appear as symbols; not in the sense of mere figures which refer to some given reality by means of suggestion and allegorical renderings, but in the sense of forces each of which produces and posits a world of its own. In these realms the spirit exhibits itself in that inwardly determined dialectic by virtue of which alone there is any reality, any organized and definite Being at all. Thus the special symbolic forms are not imitations, but organs of reality, since it is solely by their agency that anything real becomes an object for intellectual

apprehension, and as such is made visible to us. The question as to what reality is apart from these forms, and what are its independent attributes, becomes irrelevant here.[12]

This move inward, coupled with the idea of cultural evolution, borrowed from the English anthropologists, and the idea of the centrality of language, borrowed from Max Mueller, govern Cassirer's theory of myth.

The realms of science, religion, and common sense are not, says Cassirer, given to us as already structured realities to which we assign names as labels. These worlds are the latter-day products of a process of differentiation out of a globally apprehended whole. As language evolves, it divides, determines, fixates, and generalizes in the course of creating a world. Thought develops from mythic thinking, which limits, concentrates, compresses, telescopes, and hypostatizes experience, to theoretical thinking, which expands, distributes, generalizes, and systematically connects experience. Thought and language mutually influence each other; a change in one is reflected in a change in the other. Their progress can best be detected in the correlative development of religious thought from mana/tabu (a prelinguistic distinction), to momentary gods, to special gods, to personal gods, to the identity beyond language of Atman (the generalized self) with Brahman (the generalized world). All the higher forms of thought have their origin in the matrix of myth, whose metaphors are no mere decoration or allegory but a fundamental condition of language.

From the first, however, language contains the capacity for logic. As a consequent, mythic thought is destined to become mere art as it is superseded by a thought pursuing to the very limits of language the goal of rationally explaining reality. In this respect Cassirer embraces the intellectualism of Tyler, Lang, and Frazer. Ultimately, all the forms of word and image—science as well as myth—are recognized by mind "for what they really are: forms of its own self-revelation."[13] Myth, then, is about the self as consciousness.

**Claude Lévi-Strauss: Myth as Mediator Between Culture and Nature.**   To Lévi-Strauss (1908–), the study of mythology is in disarray and needs to be made scientific. That requires a search for the invariant element in myth. As an anthropologist who did fieldwork, he observed that societies often contain internal contradictions. He theorized that myths are imaginary tales which attempt to resolve such binary oppositions, often between culture and nature, by means of a special logic. Contrary to what others—principally, Lucien Levy-Bruhl—have said, this logic is every bit as rigorous as our own. For two opposed terms incapabable of mediation, mythic logic substitutes a set of equivalent opposites which do permit mediation. The process of substitution and mediation may be repeated until the original contradiction disappears from view and the sense of contradiction exhausted. For example, in Greek society there existed a contradiction arising from the traditional cosmology, on the one hand, which said that humans are autochthonous (born from the earth), and experience, on the other, which showed that humans come from humans. In the Oedipus trilogy, which is intended to deal with this contradiction, the autochthonous versus nonautochthonous opposition is replaced by another, the overvaluing of blood relations versus the undervaluing of blood relations, which is mediated by Oedipus, who partakes of the former (he marries his mother) as well as the latter (he kills his father). In the myths of many oral societies the trickster figure plays the same role.

So far, Lévi-Strauss's theory could be classified as functionalist and assigned, along with Malinowski, to the outside middle; however, his structuralism must be taken into account. The elements of the story representing binary oppositions do not appear when the myth is read diachronically (according to their order in the narrative) but only when they are grouped according to common themes (synchronically) and the groups are set against each other. These oppositions are mythic structures which, in turn, reflect deeper structures, that are like a system of grammatical rules. The deep structures generate the superstructures, which embody the particular content of the myth. Only the former are of genuine interest to Lévi-Strauss. They are the invariant which his deliberately scientific approach seeks; expressed as rules, they are analogous to scientific laws. The deep structures, in their turn, actually reflect the patterns of structuring activity inherent in the human mind. This is a universal, collective mind operating behind and expressing itself through the individual consciousness of a myth's author. When to this view is added the notion, borrowed from Saussurean semiotics, that the relation between a sign (a word and its meaning, in this instance) and its referent (the reality to which the meaning refers) is arbitrary, it is clear that for Lévi-Strauss, myth is actually about an inside, the human mind. As a means of

<!-- margin annotation: autochthonous -->

understanding the universe, myth is an illusion. Because myth is seen as an attempt to solve intellectual problems by means of logic, the theory is inside up. It is a collectivist version of Cassirer's neo-Kantian idealism and a kind of phenomenological noetics along linguistic lines.

## Inside Middle

**Rudolf Bultmann: Myths as Possibilities for Human Existence.** The inner-outer dichotomy is in the forefront of Bultmann's (1884–1976) approach to myth. The outer world is the world of space and time, a closed, mechanical system operating according to causal laws. The inner world is the realm of selfhood. Here, the ego acquires understandings and makes decisions affecting human existence understood as a temporal project directed toward the future. Each world has its own kind of thinking. The outside requires objective detachment, the method used by science and scientific history. The inside demands subjective involvement. The emphasis upon choices and decisions points to that dimension of human personality traditionally designated by "will." Since will is sometimes said to be less important than the intellect and to operate beneath the intellect and, therefore, lower on the ontological hierarchy, I identify Bultmann's theory as inside middle.

*[margin note: will beneath intellect]*

Once the distinctions above are drawn, Bultmann says that myth uses the language of the world of space and time to speak about the subjective world of the self. Problems of credibility, consequently, arise for us in the modern world as a result of our mistakenly assuming that myths are about objective realities. The remedy is not to abandon myths but to demythologize them—that is, to interpret them in terms of existential self-understanding. When we do so, we see that myths are actually about human hopes, fears, anxieties, intentions, actions, decisions, etc., with respect to birth, life, and death. In theological terms, they are about guilt, repentance, faith, obedience, and self-transformation. In principle, all mythological statements can be demythologized in this fashion.

Applied to Christianity, this means that eschatology is about God's temporal transcendence, the emptiness and unreality of the world, and human insecurity in the face of the future. The creation story in Genesis is not primitive cosmology but an expression of human dependence upon God. Finally, the resurrection of Jesus is

not about the resuscitation of a physical body but the recovery of
faith by the disciples, who had lost it following the crucifixion. It is
about what is happening inside human experience.

## Inside Down

Depth psychology finds the cause and explanation of human
behavior inside the psyche but beneath the level of conscious
experience. Because of its popularity among the general populace
and among literary theorists, it has been the most influential
approach to myth in this century.

**Sigmund Freud: Myth as Repressed Libido.**   For Freud (1856–
1939), the human psyche is a kind of thermodynamic mechanism
in which libido, a generalized, mobile, pleasure-seeking energy,
successively endows the body's orifices with special sensitivity to
pleasure and pain. When the vital activities carried out through the
orifices—eating, elimination, movement, sexuality—are socially
acceptable, a person is psychologically healthy. When the behavior
is not acceptable, repression—that is, occlusion of the normal flow
of libidinal energy, takes place. Just as water pressure builds up in
a pipe when a valve is shut, so repressed energy builds up in the
subconscious, a storeroom for the asocial contents of the personality, causing pathological consequences. The id (subconscious
forces) continues to try to express itself but, fearing further repression, does so in disguised or symbolic forms intended to elude cen-
sorship by the superego, that part of consciousness which internal-
izes social norms. For an individual, these symbolic expressions
are dreams; myths are public, collective dreams. Myths and
dreams, then, carry the neurotic contents of the subconscious.
Since the aim of therapy is to effect a permanent emptying of
repressed material from the subconscious, it follows that a thoroughly healthy person will have no need of myth.
   Freud reaches the same conclusions when his theory is applied
to culture. Like others influenced by Darwin, he saw culture as
developing from magic to religion to science, stages which parallel
the development from childhood to youth to adulthood. Out-
growing myth, then, is a necessary condition of cultural maturity.

**Carl Jung: Myth as Archetypal Meaning.**   For Jung (1875–1961),
as for Freud, the actual meaning of myth is the depths of the self, in
particular the contents of the unconscious viewed positively, even

religiously. For Jung, consciousness is a tiny island in the midst of the vast and ineradicable unconscious. The latter consists of two parts. The personal unconscious contains the forgotten experiences of the individual from birth onward, while the collective unconscious runs backward through the entire history and evolution of the human race. This forgotten past is preserved in the form of archetypes, inherited tendencies like a bird's instinct to build a nest and rooted in preestablished patterns in the brain. Ancient in origin, these archetypes, only some of which have been identified, continue to express themselves spontaneously in thoughts, feelings, and actions. The archetypes are never directly seen but are inferred from their manifestations—namely, the universal and typical symbols found in myth and other forms of literature.

Jung's approach may be illustrated by a partial interpretation of the German fairy tale, "The Princess in the Tree."[14] It tells of a swineherd who climbs a tree into the clouds to free a princess from captivity. After several dangerous encounters with a magical hunter, a witch, and a raven, the pair escape, he on a three-legged horse and she on a four-legged one. Later, the horses themselves turn into a prince and a princess. In the Jungian interpretation each figure in the story is examined, clarified, and generalized. Three-leggedness is separated from the horse and raised to the principle of threeness. Applying the Axiom of Maria, borrowed from the history of mythology and alchemy, one discovers that threeness is masculine. The swineherd's horse, however, was a mare. By plugging these facts into Jung's theory of the psyche, one can see that the three-legged mare is the animus or masculine principle in a woman, one of the identified archetypes of the collective unconscious. A similar analysis of each figure in the story reveals that the tale is about the effort of a swineherd to climb to the realm of spirit and free his captured anima (his feminine principle) and to become integrated into a whole person at the level of spirit.

Perhaps because depth psychology is of more recent origin than some of the other approaches and because it is more remote from traditional and commonsense views, it insists most strongly on the inner-outer dichotomy. Robert Johnson, using the Parsifal story and Jungian thought to create a theory of male psychology, is a case in point. He cautions:

> For, as we observed, the myth is not talking here about an outer, flesh-and-blood woman when it speaks of Blanche Fleur, but

about man's inner woman, his anima. *It is terribly important to make this distinction* between the outer, flesh-and-blood woman and a man's inner feminine quality, and to keep inner laws differentiated from the outer laws. The laws of the psyche, the laws that pertain inwardly, are unique and often different from the outer laws.[15] (emphasis mine)

He goes on to warn against confusing inner and outer and to say that the inner is what is important.

## PROBLEMS WITH MODERN MYTH THEORIES

What are we to make of these modern theories of myth? There are, of course, standard criticisms of the several views. A short list of them includes the following: that Malinowski's pragmatic theory ignores genuine intellectual concerns among "primitives" and that he generalized from a single case (the Trobriand Islanders); that Tylor, Lang, Freud, and Cassirer were mistaken in believing culture evolved through fixed stages; that Lewis places too much faith in reason and confuses myth and history; that Bultmann demythologizes only to remythologize and that his hermeneutics of the Bible is too dependent upon Heidegger's philosophy; that the theories of Lévi-Strauss and Jung are ahistorical; that Freud's theory is reductionistic and deterministic; and, versus Freud and Jung, that myths are not simply public dreams but reflect artistic workmanship.

My question, however, is about these theories as a group and what they share in common as products of modernity. If the classification scheme outlined above properly describes them, what are we to make of them and of the bifurcation of inner and outer? While Cassirer, Bultmann, and Johnson regard it as indispensable, other thinkers are less sanguine about the split. Joseph Campbell, on the one hand, analyzes the writings of Thomas Mann and James Joyce as paradigmatic of the creation of personal myths by making an inward journey. The "key" to their progression "lies in the stress on what is inward." On the other hand, he issues the following qualification:

The outward occasions represent, however, substantial external contexts of their own, of historical, socio-political, and economic relationships—to which, in fact, the intellects of the minor characters of these novels are generally addressed. And that such relationships have force, and even make claims on the loyalties of the protagonists, not only is recognized, but is fundamental to the arguments of the adventures. In the words of Joyce's hero: "When the soul of a man is born in this country there are nets flung at it to hold it back from flight. You talk to me of nationality, language, religion. I shall try to fly by those nets." Obviously, an outward-directed intellect, recognizing only such historical ends and claims, would be very much in danger of losing touch with its natural base, becoming involved wholly in the realization of "meanings" parochial to its local time and place. But, on the other hand, anyone hearkening only inward to the dispositions of feeling, would be in equal danger of losing touch with the only world in which he would ever have the possibility of living as a human being.[16]

Campbell goes on to commend Joyce and Mann for holding the inner and outer in "balanced correlation," although Joyce's reference to "nets" makes clear that the outer amounts to a series of alien constraints.

Psychologist Ira Progoff analyzes filmmaker Ingmar Bergman as an example of creative persons who produce an "inner myth of personality."

The creative person is one who is able to draw upon the images within himself and then to embody them in outer works, moving inward again and again for the inspiration of new source material, and outward again and again to learn from his artwork what it wants to become while he is working on it.[17]

The integrity of the artist depends on this "dialectical process" in which the inner and outer worlds continue to communicate with each other. Ironically, the call for communication or balance between the two worlds has the effect of reaffirming the existence of distinct realities. When Progoff notes that "these outer works are equally as symbolic as the contents of sleep dreams," his solution takes on the character of a displacement of the outer by an invasion from the inner.

The opposite tack is taken by Lévi-Strauss, who, instead of making the outer into an inner, makes the inner into an outer. Speaking of the "schism" between scientific and mythical thinking (outside and inside, respectively), he reports his impression that "contemporary science is tending to overcome this gap." As an example, he points out that scientists' discovery that various

smells have distinctive chemical compositions has made objective
what was previously believed to be merely subjective.[18] This
implies a solution in which the inner/outer dichotomy is overcome
as the inner is transformed into the outer by the advance of science. The meaning of "outer," however, remains defined in terms
of the dichotomy; hence, the dichotomy is not really eliminated.
Indeed, with the exception of the integration of psychology and
sociology by some theorists, a move prepared for by the function-
alism of the social sciences, in which it was easy enough to accommodate variant theories by adding another function, the situation
remains largely unchanged.

Each of these theories, then, insofar as it claims to be a comprehensive one, is reductionistic and is pitted methodologically
against all the others. More recently, however, William Doty's
*Mythography: The Study of Myths and Rituals*, which he intends
to be "an English-language bibliographic resource" of current theories about myth and ritual, criticizes such "monomythic definitions" and proposes instead a polyfunctional view.[19] He offers the
following "comprehensive working definition" of myth:

> A mythological corpus consists of (1) a usually complex net-
> work of myths that are (2) culturally important (3) imaginal (4)
> stories, conveying by means of (5) metaphoric and symbolic dic-
> tion, (6) graphic imagery, and (7) emotional conviction and par-
> ticipation, (8) the primal, foundational accounts (9) of aspects
> of the real, experienced world and (10) humankind's roles and
> relative statuses within it.
>
> Mythologies may (11) convey the political and moral values
> of a culture and (12) provide systems of interpreting (13) indi-
> vidual experiences within a universal perspective, which may
> include (14) the intervention of suprahuman entities as well as
> (15) aspects of the natural and cultural orders. Myths may be
> enacted or reflected in (16) rituals, ceremonies, and dramas, and
> (17) they may provide materials for secondary elaboration, the
> constituent mythemes having become merely images or refer-
> ence points for a subsequent story, such as a folktale, historical
> legend, novella, or prophecy.[20]

He sees this definition

> . . . as a step toward an inclusive matrix for understanding many
> types of myths, myths that function differently within different
> social settings yet share a sufficient number of common features
> among those of the definition to be recognizable as "myth."[21]

In subsequent chapters I intend to argue against specific elements of his definition. For the moment, however, I will limit myself to a few general remarks. I share Doty's hope for a comprehensive understanding of myth and admire greatly his effort, in the face of great obstacles, to provide one. His adoption of a polyfunctional definition reflects the authentic insight that many disciplines, perhaps all of them, have a contribution to make to myth studies.

Polyfunctionality, however, is a rather blunt instrument; its logic is merely additive. It achieves comprehensiveness, if and when it does, largely by merely tacking on to the current list of enumerated functions the latest entry into the field. It does little or nothing to bring about coherence, let alone unity, among those functions. It gathers disparate people under one roof but can do little or nothing to lure them out of their separate rooms, much less get them to talk to each other, and even less to get them to reach agreement.

Moreover, polyfunctionality operates at an abstract level and, consequently, skates above a host of significant differences. The actual theories of myth upon which Doty comments in the bulk of his book are often outright contradictory and, in any case, their methodological—not to mention ontological—fracture lines do not line up for an easy blending. This is most easily seen when considering the anthropological implications of these theories. The biological determinism of a Freud cannot be made harmonious with the existentialist freedom of a Bultmann or the intellectualist idealism of a Cassirer, for example. Nearly all myth theories make ontological or anthropological claims, and even those which do not have ontological implications.

Doty seems to have little interest in the ontology or epistemology of the myth theories he surveys or at least little interest in a radical critique directed at those topics. Perhaps this is because his interest in myth is primarily literary. It is also possible that Doty's own ontology is in essential agreement with that of modernity. Although he asserts that myth is a "particular kind of fiction," he goes to great pains to point out that "fictional" cannot in all cases be equated with "unreal." Later on, however, he claims that mythic meanings are "'invented' and 'fictionalized' onto the world."[22] Even if one takes into account his qualifications about "fictive," it seems clear that for him, as for other exponents of the inside, myth is a subjective projection of the psyche. Indeed, its function today is "that of modeling possible personal roles and concepts of the self."[23]

Early on, he states that one of the purposes of his book is to question the opposition between myth and science, but later he does not include science. He locates sacred myth, philosophical reflection, fables, anecdotes, poems, and novels in the "'fictional' range of a culture."[24] Given his definition, this omission cannot be because science is not fictional; instead, I suspect, it reflects Doty's acritical acceptance, after all, of the reality of the modern scientific worldview as a counterpoint to understanding myth. I wish to make clear that I do not claim that Doty explicitly subscribes to either metaphysical dualism or the epistemological dualism based on it. Most recent thinkers, I would estimate, reject these as doctrines. What remains, however, is a critical rhetoric and a set of intellectual standards based on dualism. It is a nearly inescapable, tacit reliance upon this Cartesian legacy, which so often undermines the good intentions of myth critics and others. This explains the strange reversals noted above in Doty's theory. Finally, he refers to "persons in a society where myths are very much alive and strongly determinative of everyday actions,"[25] as if there are persons, perhaps himself among them, whose lives are now myth-free.

By itself, polyfunctionality leaves intact the inner-outer dichotomy of modernity and perpetuates the cultural schizophrenia with which we have been too long afflicted. If nature and society are objective, then all attempts at finding a meaning to sustain human existence in the world are destined from the outset to be abortive. Alternatively, if human meaning is a mere matter of the inside, then that meaning is a subjective illusion without anchorage in nature, history, and society.

In the end, the modern rescuers of myth, and even the rescuers of the rescuers, have too little to show for their efforts. They succeeded in demonstrating, contrary to the thinkers of the Enlightenment, that myth makes a kind of sense and is worth serious study. That's all to the good. On the other hand, consistent with their modern presuppositions, they view myth as associated with what is primitive, past, subjective, and untrue—namely, all the things that modernity hopes to outdistance. Even when they acknowledge that myth persists among persons of a nontraditional outlook, it is understood as a subjective fantasy projected onto a reality more properly defined by science.

It should be obvious that such a view, if communicated by whatever means to an oral society impressed with the gadgets of modern technology, would have precisely the effect observed among our New Guinea natives. Doubtless wishing to preserve New Guinea myth as a quaint curiosity, Carpenter took no action deliberately intended to stamp it out. On the other hand, believing, most likely, that moderns have evolved beyond myth, he could do nothing to nurture its vitality. New Guinea myth was left neither quite dead nor fully alive, but numb.

In the chapters that follow I intend to steer a different course. In Chapter 3 I will examine theories in which myth is admitted to exist in modernity but which seem to exempt part of modernity from mythic influence. In Chapter 4 I will argue that not only is myth alive and well but that it is situated in the very heart of modernity, including natural science. Only when we can acknowledge that myth is good enough to keep company with us in our most advanced thinking, indeed, only when we can acknowledge our indispensable dependence upon it, are we likely to take myth seriously enough truly to understand and appreciate it. In Chapter 5, using insights from Michael Polanyi and the existential phenomenology of Maurice Merleau-Ponty, I will attempt to set forth a postcritical, as opposed to poststructural or postmodern, understanding of myth, one in which the dichotomy of inner and outer is exorcised, at least to the present limits of my insights.

TABLE 1.
Chart of Modern Myth Theories

| *Inside Up* | *Outside Up* |
|---|---|
| Discipline: Philosophy | Discipline: Theology |
| School: Idealism | Object: God |
| Self: Intellect | Examples:  J. R. R. Tolkien |
| Examples:  Ernst Cassirer | C. S. Lewis |
| Claude Lévi-Strauss | Clark Pinnock |
| | Carl F. H. Henry |

| *Inside Middle* | *Outside Middle* |
|---|---|
| Discipline: Philosophy | Discipline:  Sociology |
| School: Existentialism | Anthropology |
| Self: Will | Object: Society, Culture |
| Examples:  Rudolf Bultmann | Examples: B. Malinowski |
| Paul Brockelman | |

| *Inside Down* | *Outside Down* |
|---|---|
| Discipline:  Psychology | Discipline:  Philology |
| Literature | Anthropology |
| School: Psychoanalysis | Object: Nature |
| Self: Feelings | Examples:  Max Mueller |
| Examples:  Sigmund Freud | E.B. Tylor |
| Carl Jung | Andrew Lang |
| Joseph Campbell | James Frazer |
| Ira Progoff | |
| James Hillman | |

Bultman— one has to understand the significance of Jesus
as an inner experience
No one experienced the resurrection
There was no physical resurrection
Important was the empty tomb

# CHAPTER 3

# *Myth at the Margins of Modernity*

Almost from the moment that theories of myth arose in Greece, simultaneously and necessarily reflectively distinguishing myth from other forms of thought and other modes of being, the West has been reluctant to acknowledge even the presence of myth, much less a dependence on it.[1] In that regard Western intellectual history can be read as a long retreat before the advance of myth, a retreat slowed by the following delaying tactics: (1) myth is in them, not us (the Christian apologists); (2) myth was in us, but a long time ago (Tylor, Lang, Malinowski); (3) myth was in us until quite recently when we finally began to outgrow it (Voltaire and other Enlightenment thinkers); (4) myth is in us now, but only in religion (Bultmann, Cassirer); (5) myth is in us now in a variety of spheres (religion, politics, popular culture, the collective unconscious, etc.), but not in science. Modernity has had particular difficulty in admitting its "defilement" by myth because expunging myth from Western culture—a necessary condition for the attainment of certainty—was a central aim of its program. More recently, however, a few thinkers have begun to consider the impossible—namely, that particular aspects of modern thought have an intimate connection to myth. As modern theories, they can, like the theories in Chapter 2, be analyzed in terms of the categories inside, outside, up, down, and middle. It is, however, the respect in which they differ from those previous theories—namely, in their willingness to acknowledge modernity itself as containing myth, that I wish now to consider.

## MYTH AT THE MARGINS OF MODERN THOUGHT

### Mircea Eliade: Myth as Collective Participation in Common Symbols

One of the most prolific writers on the subject of myth is historian of religion Mircea Eliade. For him myth is a special form of collective thinking, of collective participation in common symbols. His investigations, which were directed almost entirely to the myths of preliterate societies, led him to detect "survivals" of traditional myths in modern society. The most obvious of these is Christianity, which continues to propagate "the mode of being of archaic man." More typical of modernity, however, are a number of political and social mythologies. Because they are laicized and secularized, their character as myths is camouflaged. Among these are Marxism, whose founder, Karl Marx,

> ... takes up and carries on one of the great eschatological myths of the Middle Eastern and Mediterranean world, namely: the redemptive part played by the Just (the "elect," the "anointed," the "innocent," the "missioners", in our own days by the proletariat), whose sufferings are invoked to change the ontological status of the world.[2]

The classless society is but a modern version of the myth of the Golden Age. National Socialism, on the other hand, promoted the myth of the Aryan as both primordial Ancestor and noble Hero. Collective participation in the celebrations of the New Year, the birth of a child, and the building of a house are enactments of the myth of new beginnings. Education and didactic teaching are secularized versions of functions formerly carried out by myth. Finally, the media, sporting events, and such pastimes as reading (comic books, poetry, and novels) put before us archetypal heroes (Superman) and replay ancient themes (good versus evil).

*Taylor Stevenson: History as Myth*

Perhaps the most direct challenge to modernity's rejection of myth was mounted by Taylor Stevenson, who took advantage of the following widely accepted fivefold definition of "myth" put forward by Eliade:

1. Myths are the actions of the Supernaturals in *illo tempore*.
2. Myths are true and sacred because about realities.
3. Myths are related to a creation or origin and provide models to be imitated and recovered by anamnesis.
4. By knowing the myths about anything's origin, one can control it.
5. One lives the myth, transcending profane time.[3]

In a move anticipated by Eliade, Stevenson argues that history is myth because it fulfills the definition above. This is possible when human beings are regarded as the "Supernaturals" in that they are the creators and rulers of history. History is the true account of reality, relating the origin of our institutions and offering paradigms for significant human actions. Quoting Eliade, Stevenson says that one "lives" the myth of history "in the sense that one is seized by the sacred, exalting power of the events recollected or re-enacted."[4] Although Stevenson himself does not do so, one could make use of Eliade to speak, as others have done, of the Myth of Reason. In that instance the pre-Socratics would become the "Supernaturals."

## Michael Novak: Myths as Guiding Images, Symbols, and Values

One of the most forceful efforts to demonstrate the presence of myth in the modern world is that of Michael Novak. He did not identify myth with any particular idea, such as history or reason or evolution, but saw it as a complex of images, symbols, and values which govern our thinking and doing. To make his point he invented several fictional characters, one of whom is a believer in progress.

> Take, for example, John Leotard, book reviewer for a major national magazine. He thinks of himself as an atheist, and he profoundly hates the complacency and pious moral certainty of the religious people he grew up with. . . . Freedom, he thinks, means having the courage to face the void. But there is a paradox in his behavior. He is rather righteous about liberal causes; indignant at stupidity, injustice, fraud; eager to lend his energies whenever he can to the forces of progress and enlightenment. He hates the yahoos. On the other hand, he seems to claim that everything is relative, that no one knows for certain what is right or true, that we are lost in a vast darkness, that men are, like Prometheus, noblest when they hurl against their fate a thundering No! . . . The fact is that Leotard has a way of picking out what is real in human experience and leaving behind what is insignificant, sham, unworthy of notice. He imagines himself living out a story of freedom, honesty, courage—of heresy, enlightenment, heroic dissent—in the vanguard of cultural advance. He alternates between exalting modern society (his heroes led the breakthroughs which made it possible: Voltaire, Hume, Paine, Russell) and excoriating what business-

men and bureaucrats have made of it. One of his favorite symbols is that of the lonely outsider, the dissenter, the powerless cultural heretic persecuted for his superior honesty and insight, opening the path for future generations. . . . In a word, Leotard has a quite defined standpoint from which to experience, understand, and act; a direction; a sense of where he stands in relation to other persons and, indeed, to universal history; screens of perception; and criteria of judgment. He belongs to no church or organization; recites no creed; takes part in no established rituals. Except that cocktail parties, openings, publication days, tendencies, trends, and causes give his life every bit as much symbolic significance and shape as any churchgoer gains.[5]

Novak goes on to say of Leotard and others like him that:

Their basic sense of reality derives from "reason" or "scientific method" or "modern consciousness." Their basic story is that of evolutionary progress, especially through knowledge and social reform. Their basic symbols are Prometheus, Sisyphus, the Nobel or Pulitzer prize; "reason," "enlightenment," "freedom," "social justice," "honesty," "relativism," "process," and the like. They take as their task the dissolution and criticism of what is, in the name of a better world to come, or (if they are cynical about "progress") in the name of fearless honesty.[6]

Eliade, Stevenson, and Novak, along with a handful of others of whom I have chosen these three as representative, deserve credit for honesty in owning up to the presence of myth in modernity and for understanding myth to influence thought as well as action; nevertheless, their theories are neither satisfactory nor persuasive. All of them so radically redefine "myth" as to make it unrecognizable and, consequently, sharply diminish the significance of their effort. Myth becomes equated with symbol (cross), image (the damned artist), value (freedom), theme (new beginnings), or role model (Superman). Perhaps this indifference to form stems from the functionalist orientation, once so pervasive, which says, in effect, what functions like X, is X. Eliade claims, for example, that "the function of a national flag, with all the affective experiences that go with it, was *in no way different* from the 'participation' in any of the symbols of archaic societies (emphasis mine)."[7] This is an uncritically held and dubious assumption; moreover, it is a strange claim from one who also speaks of myth as "the expression of a *mode of being in the world* (emphasis his)." It is arguable—and I will do so later—

that different forms are the expression of and vehicles for different modes of being. For Eliade it is the theme which has efficacy; the myth itself is merely the theme's vehicle. Stevenson's identification of "myth" and "history" renders both terms nonsensical; "I am now eating a hamburger" becomes logically indistinguishable from "In the beginning God created the heavens and the earth." In any case, the pragmatic collapsing together of different forms only creates more confusion where there is already too much. Finally, whereas these theories have the merit of pointing beyond the role of myth in action to its role in thinking, the thinking involved seems to be of a more practical rather than theoretical nature—that is, it is not applicable to what we regard as our highest, best, most serious thinking. Scientific thinking, especially, appears to be excluded. Myth is admitted to modernity, but, as yet, it plays only about the edges.

## MYTH AT THE MARGINS OF SCIENTIFIC THOUGHT

In the decade of the sixties the revolutionary challenges to so many aspects of the sociocultural landscape took aim at science, the ideal of knowledge in the modern age and the cultural institution in the name of which myth was to be eradicated. For perhaps the first time since Vico myth and science were linked, however peripherally and haltingly. This linkage will now be explored in a logical, rather than chronological, sequence.

### *Harvey Cox: Genesis as the Disenchantment of Nature*

Theologian Harvey Cox does not offer a general theory of myth but purports to show how one myth, the Creation story in Genesis, contributed to the rise of science, both ancient and modern. It did so by secularizing nature, both human and subhuman, thus making it an appropriate object for scientific investigation.[8]

Prior to science totemistic and animistic views of nature dominated preliterate societies, and more sophisticated versions of animism were found among the advanced civilizations of the ancient world. Animism, as we have seen, held that the rocks, fields, trees, and streams of nature were inhabited by semiautonomous spirits whose actions could affect the well-being of humankind. Totemism adds that human beings are linked by kinship to these spirits; they are our relatives. In that circumstance the most appropriate behavior toward nature is worship or coercion by magic, not detached scientific examination.

Genesis, however, functions like atheistic propaganda, countering both animism and totemism. As against the former, Genesis says that Yahweh is the creator of nature and, therefore, distinct from it. It follows that the moon, stars, plants, and animals are merely creatures and not divine beings which must be placated. Against totemism Genesis says that we are not brothers and sisters of the kangaroos and apes; instead, human beings are the progeny of other human beings. Disenchantment—that is, clearing the forests of fairies and elves—makes nature an appropriate object of scientific observation and analysis. Note that although Cox is claiming that a particular myth prepares the way for science, he makes no claim that science itself in any way involves myth.

## Stephen Toulmin: Myth as the Misuse of Scientific Results

Philosopher of science Stephen Toulmin brings modern science and myth closer together when he examines "contemporary scientific mythology."[9] In the nineteenth century, he argues, works of natural theology were popular reading for the educated public. Such books had a double purpose. On the one hand, they attempted to explain the natural order. On the other, they sought to answer pressing moral and theological questions. In the twentieth century science has replaced theology as the authority for explaining nature; consequently, the authority of the scientist has increased while the authority of the preacher has diminished. The public, however, is still interested in moral and theological issues and turns now to the scientist for help. Enamored of their status in a new priesthood, popular scientists in their "off-duty" (Toulmin's term) writings and pronouncements have yielded to these pleas for answers and in so doing have at once misled the public and deceived themselves. Possessing no special expertise, they have, nevertheless, expounded on a variety of nonscientific matters, even the unknown and unknowable remote past and future, lending to their conclusions the prestige and authority of science. The result, says Toulmin, has been the creation of scientific mythologies—that is, myths made out of scientific knowledge. These exhibit two identifying features: (1) they use scientific terms not in their precise, narrow, and purely scientific sense but in an extended sense and (2) they do so in the service of moral, theological, or philosophical purposes.

To illustrate his point Toulmin examines the myth of the "running-down universe." The myth is based on the second law of thermodynamics, according to which in a thermally isolated or closed system entropy, the amount of disorder among the elements of the system, either remains constant or increases. As entropy increases the amount of energy available for useful work decreases and the temperatures of the parts of the system will even out. Toulmin observes that the second law of thermodynamics was created in the course of determining the efficiency of steam engines operating at a certain temperature and can also be used to calculate such things as the amount of power needed to run a refrigerator. This law, applying merely to heat exchanges in a limited range of systems, is generalized, however, by "off-duty" scientists to apply to the universe as a whole. Endowed with the quality of necessity, this universal law becomes a law of the universe, according to which at some time in the future the universe will suffer an unavoidable "death by freezing." In Toulmin's parlance this fatalistic vision is scientific myth.

In criticizing this myth Toulmin notes that the universe as a whole cannot be a thermally isolated system since anything surrounding and enclosing the universe would be part of the universe itself. Moreover, if stopping the running-down universe is said to be a theoretical impossibility, we must not understand that impossibility to be like a more recalcitrant form of practical impossibility; rather, "theoretical impossibility" is a feature of the framework into which the scientific facts are fit. In Toulmin's instrumentalist view theories, after all, tell us nothing about reality; they are like tools from which we may pick and choose to achieve certain ends. In that regard theories are like various systems of map projection. For some purposes the Mercator system is most useful; for other purposes another system is better. "Theoretical impossibility" points to the limits of a particular system of "projection." For example, it is theoretically impossible to weigh fire because fire is understood to be a process rather than a substance and is, therefore, not the sort of thing which can be weighed.

Once again, however, although scientific myths contain scientific terms and are articulated by scientists themselves, true science remains untainted by myth. Scientific myths arise only from the abuse of science, not its legitimate practice.

*Michael Foster: Myths as Determinants of Scientific Method*

English philosopher Michael Foster argues that the methods employed by science are chosen in accordance with a previously held philosophy of nature, which, in turn, is based on a theology of God and creation. He himself does not mention myth. I believe no violence is done to his views by adding a step which says that a theology of God and creation is derived from an origin myth.

Foster illustrates his argument by analyzing the shift from ancient to modern science. In the composite picture painted by Foster the God of ancient Greece is a pure intellect lacking autonomous will and whose sole activity is thinking on himself. That self includes the eternal forms of all things. Nature is a composite of form and matter. Since the unchanging forms provided the models for creation, the created world is a necessary one; no other world was possible. The purely intelligible forms, however, are the real essence of nature; the material element is superfluous. It follows that perception of the material aspect of nature contributes nothing to knowledge except perhaps an assist to reason's effort to intuit the eternal form. The "intelligent comprehension of form is sufficient for the understanding of both what is and what happens in the actual world,"[10] says Foster. Scientific method, therefore, must be deductive.

Modern science appeared, on Foster's thesis, when the Reformation ousted Aristotle and promoted the Bible as the sole authority in theology. This resulted in taking seriously creation as depicted in Genesis. There Yahweh is characterized by will. Without the aid of preexisting and fixed forms, Yahweh, whose will is autonomous, creates a nature which is contingent; He could have created a different one. Moreover, because form and matter are created simultaneously and primordially together, nature is not composite but unitary. As a consequence, the material element is not superfluous and perception of the world is necessary in order to know it. Even God, whose will, in the absence of eternal forms, "exceeds determination by reason," must await the completion and observation of creation before pronouncing it good. Scientific method, therefore, must be empirical.

With Foster the relation between myth and science is more legitimate than with Toulmin and more intimate than with either Toulmin or Cox. Myth is the source of methodological presuppositions on which scientific investigations proceed. This understanding, however, has not enhanced the status of myth. This kind of influence of myth on science is too easily seen as an event in past intellectual history, a history with which neither scientific laypersons nor scientists themselves are likely to be acquainted. Beyond that, cognizance of the mythical or theological foundations of methodological assumptions is not essential to the daily practice of science. Finally, one might argue that by whatever logically or scientifically illegitimate means modern science arose, it has proven its truth and value by means of its results.

*Langdon Gilkey: Myths as Multivalent Symbols of the Transcendent*

One of the most extended and thoughtful treatments of myth is found in Langdon Gilkey's *Religion and the Scientific Future: Reflections on Myth, Science, and Theology*. He acknowledges a heavy debt to Mircea Eliade, whose characterization of ancient myth he modifies for application to the present. The result is the following definition:

> Myths to us, then, are not just ancient and thus untrue fables; rather, they signify a certain perennial mode of language, whose elements are multivalent symbols, whose referent is in some strange way the transcendent or sacred, and whose meanings concern the ultimate existential issues of actual life and the questions of human and historical destiny.[11]

Multivalent, polysemous language permits myth to speak about both finite, particular features of the phenomenal world and of the transcendent or sacred which is manifested through them. Traditional myths, which were the prototypes of philosophical, theological, historical, and scientific reflection, have been enervated in the modern era not by the shearing off of the transcendent layer of meaning so much as by empirical science's wresting from myth the control of the phenomenal. Without any grounding in nature or history myth becomes merely a symbol and empty. This outcome does not, nevertheless, leave us mythless. Taking his cue again from Eliade, he says that the two modern global and "cosmic" myths are Marxism and Evolution, although their importance has waned in this century.

Gilkey's more original contribution, however, is to speak of myth in terms of the religious dimensions of secular, scientific culture. He does so in two ways. First, he employs Michael Polanyi, Thomas Kuhn, and Alfred North Whitehead to paint a picture of scientific knowing as human, passionate, creative, willed, and autonomous, rather than objective and impersonal. In at least three ways such acts of scientific knowing contain hints of ultimacy. (1) They are grounded in and made possible by wonder and a passion to know, which drive one on despite obstacles, wrong turns, and blind alleys and, because of their disregard for the consequences of knowing, are, paradoxically, the basis for disinterestedness. (2) Scientific knowing also starts from unverified and unverifiable presuppositions, global visions, and theories which guide it. (3) Finally, there are hints of ultimacy in the self-affirmation of rational judgments, which, amazingly and mysteriously, triumph over corrosive doubt, an infinity of internal relations in the world, and endless qualifications to achieve the unconditioned "it is so" of finite truth. Gilkey's claim is that mythical language alone is adequate to speak of these elements of ultimacy.

Secondly, Gilkey argues that myth is actually present in a new species of "postmodern" anthropocentric myths. These gnostic myths speak of the creative, rational, and autonomous powers of humans. Exhibiting the common features of all myths, they use multivalent language to speak of transcendence (the transcendent powers of humans), they talk about ultimate destiny and meaning, and they provide models and norms for social behavior. The prime example of this new breed of myths is "the myth of the new scientific man." This man wears a white coat, knows the secret structures of things and can control them, and can create not only a new environment but also a new man who is free of all impediments to his will and is perfectly fulfilled. In short, scientific humans, in the words of Dr. Glenn Seaborg, can "control and direct our future, our creative evolution" and are "the masters of our fate."[12]

Gilkey is hardly sanguine about this myth, which he calls false, morally dangerous, and contradictory. It assumes that technology can be controlled, that it leads to no problems for the environment or people, and that the scientists in power are free of greed and corruption. The contradiction appears in the contrast between the image of the scientist as free, autonomous, and creative in acts of scientific knowing and in the application of science, on the one hand, and of all persons as subject to and wholly determined by a nexus of impersonal causes, on the other. For Gilkey, a corrected and deepened mythology is essential not only as the only way to solve these problems but also as the only way to give humans confidence in their destiny, including the destiny of scientific culture itself.

In many ways Gilkey's theory is the most insightful we have encountered so far and is deserving of a more careful criticism than I can give it here. I will limit myself to the observation that with respect to traditional myths Gilkey either confines their influence to the past or judges their theological descendants to have been rendered ineffectual by science. As for his postmodern anthropocentric myths, his own conclusions about them are almost entirely negative.

### Edward Maziarz: Myth and Science as Formal Symbolic Structures

Following a course between the extremes of sharply distinguishing myth and science, on the one hand, and identifying them completely, on the other, Maziarz deliberately ignores pragmatic, semantic, and functional issues in order to focus on formal similarities between the two. His assumption that myths are neither illogical nor prelogical but logical achievements of great significance puts him in Lévi-Strauss's camp in the latter's debate with Levy-Bruhl. The argument is divided into two parts.

First, Maziarz claims that myth made a positive contribution to the rise of science. Myth launched the search, later to be taken over by science, for "the ultimate properties, powers, and dispositions of matter that serve as the controllers of matter itself" as well as for "the formal and logical structures and entities perfigured (*sic*) in mythological language itself," whereby the success of the former can be assessed.[13]

Next, Maziarz rejects the view that myth's historical influence on science no longer persists. Relying on sociology, he notes that the scientific community is similar to a tribe, having its own initiation rites, its beliefs in the magic power of its own language, and its ways of distinguishing the scientists in good standing from the ones who are taboo. Moreover, both ancient and contemporary peoples use the "logos" of a variety of logico-grammatical forms both in their myths and science and in their everyday lives. In other words, the transcending of the phenomenal world by symbolic forms, begun by myth in the past, perdures in contemporary science.

These arguments lead Maziarz to a number of conclusions: (1)

that neither scientists nor mythmakers believe reality is self-explanatory, (2) that both create symbolic realities to explain the phenomenal, (3) that myths and science show man as a theorist, who creates formal patterns transcending in significance both space and time.

Maziarz does not deliver, however, on his promise to discuss the differences between science and myth. This is not surprising in view of his ruling out at the outset matters of meaning, function, and content. Moreover, while his claim about the historical influence of myth on science is straightforward, his claim about a continuing influence is not. It depends upon too great a readiness to equate the formal similarities between myth and science with a causal relation between the two while, at the same time, ignoring millennia of intervening history. Also, his claim that grammar and logic are a "necessary presupposition" of myths, science, and everyday life is, at the least, ambiguous. He cannot mean that rules of grammar and logic existed prior to the creation of myth, science, and everyday life or that people were aware of them. Perhaps he simply means that rules of grammar and logic were subsequently derived from the language of myth and science—he does not demonstrate that that is the case with myth—but that does not mean that the rules were found in determinate form already present but hidden in those languages. Such rules are created rather than discovered, even if afterward they are seen as having been prefigured in language. Finally, even if he is correct about logic and grammar, the import may be trivial, except as a response to Lévy-Bruhl. Exhibiting logic and grammar are necessary features of any serious language and, therefore, do little to illuminate the connection between any two particular languages—for example, the languages of myth and science.

### Earl MacCormac: Myth as Mistaking a Metaphor for Literal Truth

Like a number of other thinkers who set out to compare science and religion,[14] Earl MacCormac takes his point of departure from Max Black's "interaction view" of metaphor.[15] In Black's illustration "man is a wolf" the juxtaposed terms "man" and "wolf" interact so as to alter our perception of both. People are seen as more wolflike, and wolves are seen as more human. MacCormac emphasizes the tension-filled character of metaphors. The tension arises from the fact that metaphors surprise us by using a familiar term in a way that is not simply novel but is also odd or even contradictory. Metaphors can be distinguished in terms of the degree of tension and surprise they produce. A metaphor which suggests shocking new possibilities for the use of a term, new analogies between a familiar context and one of which we have little or no experience, are "diaphors." Those which are relatively more expressive of experience we already possess are "epiphors." While some metaphors have a narrow and superficial range of application, "root metaphors," such as Newton's "the world is a machine" or process thought's "the world is an organism," are more fundamental and comprehensive. All metaphors, but epiphors especially, may lose their tension and "fade" into ordinary language, which consists of literal terms, produced by ostensive definitions, and dead metaphors.

Myth is the result of the mistaken attribution of reality, finality, literalness, truth, or absoluteness to a diaphoric root metaphor, which is properly understood as speculative, tentative, hypothetical, and suggestive. MacCormac notes that such a definition is not limited to the past or to religious content but applies equally to scientific theories in the present. "Atom," "force," "particle," and "angular momentum," to mention a few terms, are metaphors found in science, and Newton's theory that the world is a mechanism strictly obeying mathematical laws became a myth when it ceased to be treated as an "as if" and was taken to be a literal description. We are able to see the mythic character of scientific theories only when a new theory comes along and recasts our perspective on the old one.

It should be understood that parts of a scientific theory may, indeed, contain a great deal of truth. The theory becomes a myth only when someone falsely claims it to be *the* picture of reality. Moreover, it is possible that the tentative suggestions advanced by a root metaphor may lead to a theory which becomes so thoroughly confirmed by observations that it can be regarded as literally true and therefore avoids characterization as a myth. The heliocentric theory of the solar system is one example, but such instances are extremely rare.

MacCormac's theory connects myth more closely to science than any theory examined thus far. He does so, however, as he himself admits, by means of a stipulative definition of "myth" which assaults common sense. His point that both scientists and scientific laypersons mistakenly regard scientific theories as final is well-taken, but why not simply warn against taking any theory, scientific or theological, literally? Turning that point into a theory of myth is an unnecessary complication. The reason he does so is that his ultimate aim is to demonstrate the legitimacy of religious and theological language. If science contains myth and metaphor, he argues, then one cannot object if religion does too. This approach ignores significant differences between science and myth; it emphasizes too strongly the explanatory function of myth popular in the nineteenth century; and hardly takes the reader beyond the view, current among Enlightenment thinkers and in today's ordinary discourse, of myth as falsehood. Myth is accorded only instrumental value as a weapon with which to attack excessive claims about scientific knowledge.[16]

What, then, do these efforts to find myth in modernity amount to? They certainly represent an advance over the centuries old habit of seeing the two as antithetical. That is no small gain. Beyond that, however, there may be little of lasting value. Consider that the theories discussed in this chapter take one of three approaches: (1) myth prepared the way for modernity and science (Cox, Foster, Gilkey), (2) myth is identical with some aspect of modernity (Eliade, Stevenson, Novak, Toulmin, Gilkey, MacCormac, and Gerhart and Russell), or (3) myth and modernity (science), if viewed sufficiently abstractly, share certain formal analogies (Maziarz). The first approach implies that myth does not affect or "infect" modernity today or centrally. The second depends largely upon stipulative definitions that seem to make words meaningless and test our credulity. The third appears to be of relatively little significance. Indeed, such efforts as are represented in this chapter are now hardly seen. The emphasis in myth studies seems to have shifted to literature and the social sciences.

In the remaining chapters, among the things I wish to show, by contrast to the views heretofore considered, are (1) that myth does not lie outside or on the periphery of modernity but at its heart, (2) that myth's effect is not confined to the past but is operative in the present, (3) that myth is not false but has a much more complicated relation to truth and falsity, (4) that myth is not to be identified per se with any isolated feature of modernity, (5) that myth is not simply a matter of subjective self-understanding, and (6) that myth is not metaphorical. In short, I wish to sketch a theory of myth not founded on the inner-outer distinction.

# CHAPTER 4

# *Myth in the Heart of Modernity*

> These Days
> Whatever you have to say, leave
> the roots on, let them
> dangle
> And the dirt
> Just to make clear
> Where they came from
>
> —Charles Olson, *Collected*
> *Poetry of Charles Olson*

In his recent *Myth and Philosophy: A Contest of Truths*, Lawrence J. Hatab argues that early Greek philosophers, far from refuting and replacing the myths of an earlier era, merely adopted a new paradigm for thought in which the mythic content was given a rationalized form.[1] He traces the continuity of mythic themes from Greek myth and religion through the epics and tragic poetry into the writings of Thales, Xenophanes, Anaximander, Heraclitus, Parmenides, Plato, and Aristotle. Much earlier, *Creation: The Impact of an Idea*, a collection of essays edited by Daniel O'Connor and Francis Oakley, examined the impact of the Christian doctrine of creation on a variety of aspects of Western civilization, including medieval technology and seventeenth-century science.[2] In his *Myth and Modern Philosophy* Stephen Daniel brings to bear hermeneutic, semiotic, poststructuralist, and deconstructive techniques to show mythic elements in the writings of seventeenth- and eighteenth-century philosophers, some of whom were overtly hostile to myth.[3]

What I wish to do in this chapter is somewhat similar to the programs of Hatab, Oakley and O'Connor, and Daniel. Unlike Hatab, however, I will look not at a distillation of many prephilosophical Greek myths but a single, later philosophical myth— namely, the account of origins in Plato's *Timaeus*.[4] At the same

hermeneutic - interpretive
semiotic - theory of signs + symbols
poststructuralist
deconstructive

time, I wish to examine not Christian doctrine but the P-account of creation in the biblical book of Genesis. I wish to show in a cursory way the pervasive influence of these two myths not only in the past but in the most sophisticated domains of the present. Their influence may be found within the walls of academia, where the theories of both science and philosophy, for example, are dependent on them.

I do not claim that these two myths, traditional in both form and content, are the only myths to affect Western culture, that only Greek and Hebrew myths have had any such effect, or that either Greek or Hebrew thought is monolithic. Athens and Jerusalem are, however, the most significant traditional roots of the West, and myths of origin aim at a comprehensiveness which gives them long arms. Finally, my argument will not be a matter of tracing historical connections so much as pointing to patterns (thematic identities, structural homologies, and common orientations) which display a family resemblance between an obviously mythic past and an obviously theoretical present.

## THE TIMAEUS

Far from suffering from the absence of myth, the West has been and is now under the spell of a particular and somewhat peculiar myth—namely, the myth of origin in Plato's *Timaeus*. As the only original work of Plato's available to European philosophers in the early middle ages and the most influential work for the neo-Pythagorean revival that helped give rise to modern science, it provided and continues to provide a fundamental orientation for much of modernity. In that myth the world is the result of the imitative activity of the Demiurge who, looking at the eternal pattern, molds matter into its likeness to produce things. Let us look at each of these elements in turn.

The eternal pattern is understood by Plato's interpreters to be none other than the Forms spoken of in his earlier writings. They are eternal and, therefore, divine. Not one of them will ever disappear from and no new ones will ever come into being. As unchanging and unchangeable patterns, they are the ground for stability, order, and necessity in the world. As intelligibilities, they are the ground and goal of all genuine knowledge. As pure intelligibilities, whose meanings are discrete (the idea of justice contains not even an ounce of injustice), they foreshadow a logic containing the principles of noncontradiction, identity, and excluded middle. Being general in nature, the Ideas make possible universality. Because they provide the pattern for the essence of made things, they impart to the world its intelligibility. Realities are knowable in the form of definitions, which capture the essences of things, and knowledge can increase by rational intuition and deduction. The Forms constitute the basis for objective knowledge, perfect knowledge, and even omniscience. Insofar as they are in their primordial nature entirely free of matter they inspire an ascetic, moral purity.

The raw material for the world consists of matter in the form of the well-known elements of earth, air, fire, and water. These elements have inherent powers which ceaselessly operate on each other without rhyme or reason. These blind fluctuations are, then, disorderly, chaotic. They take place in a receptacle or space which is itself formless so as to accommodate any and all forms. Like the transcendent intelligibilities, matter is also eternal. Because of its independent, uncreated, eternal powers, matter can resist the imposition of form and order and deny omnipotence to any other powers. Finally, matter is the basis for individuation and particularity, for which the generic Forms lack resources.

The Forms and matter are primordially distinct from each other. As such, they constitute a metaphysical dualism. Left alone, they could never interact; both are in that respect static. If there is to be a material world and if the account of its origin is to make sense at all, there must be an active principle to bring form and matter together. That role is played by the Demiurge. Called "king," "artificer," "father," and "maker," he is not an omnipotent creator of all but takes preexistent materials and shapes them into things according to preexistent patterns. Neither matter nor the patterns is derived from the Demiurge.

In his shaping activity the Demiurge employs a variety of techniques. Sometimes he seems to be a being using hands to bend or compress matter in the manner of a potter. Sometimes he mixes elements together as if he were a chemist. At still other times he is said to "persuade" matter to yield to order, as if he were a statesman. He is not, however, a creative artist but an imitative craftsman, exercising skills of a more routine sort. He has neither a name nor a personality and is only rarely mentioned in Plato's other writings. As necessary as he is for the world's origin, he seems to be a deus ex machina brought in as an afterthought to compensate for the lack of an active, connecting, ordering principle. He is more like an impersonal force in whom the reader can develop no personal interest.

The outcome of the Demiurge's skillful performance is an orderly, intelligible world of composite beings whose eternal passing in and out of existence nevertheless maintains an overall, unchanging pattern which reflects a transcendent order of eternal, rational patterns. Insofar as the flux of the material world follows unchanging patterns, time is cyclical—that is, presents an earthly approximation to eternity. Because it is the result of the relatively routine operation of a craftsman using preexistent matter and a design not of his own making, the world has the character of a manufactured product. Moreover, despite the fact that much of earlier Greek cosmogony viewed the world as an organism, if one accepts Thomas Aquinas's definition of a machine as *"partes extra partes,"* then the world of the *Timaeus* is already a kind of rudimentary mechanism millennia in advance of Newton's modern picture of mechanism as the world's mute obedience to mathematical law.

Of the several elements in the Timaeus account contributing to the origin of the world the most significant is the eternal pattern. Spanish philosopher Ortega y Gasset clearly grasps the import of the Platonic Forms.

> Socrates was the first to realize that reason is a new universe, more perfect than and superior to that which we find, spontaneously, in our environment. Visible and tangible phenomena vary incessantly, appear and vanish, pass into one another: white blackens, water evaporates, man dies. . . . It is the same in the internal world of man: desires and projects change and contradict themselves. . . . On the other hand, pure ideas, or logoi, constitute a set of immutable beings, which are perfect and precise. The idea of whiteness contains nothing but "white"; movement never becomes static; "one" is always "one," just as two is always two. . . . There was no doubt about it: true reality had been discovered; and in contrast with it the other world, that presented to us by spontaneous life, underwent an automatic depreciation.[5]

This reality, these consequences, expressed in and derived from *Timaeus* is the myth by whose spell the West has been and remains bound to this day.

## GENESIS

Perhaps the differences between the Timaeus and Genesis can best be clarified with the help of a preliterate, native American myth. Kumokums, the aboriginal being in a Modoc tale of beginnings, wondered what Tule Lake would look like if it were surrounded by land. He reached down to the bottom of the lake and drew up a handful of mud, making a pile in front of him.

> As Kumokums patted the mud, it began to spread beneath his hand, out and around him, until Tule Lake was completely surrounded by earth, and Kumokums was left sitting on a little island of mud in the middle of the water. "Well!" said Kumokums. "I didn't know it would do that."[6]

Plato's Craftsman and the Modocs' Kumokums illustrate Lévi-Strauss's distinction between the engineer, who constructs a machine from a detailed blueprint, and the "*bricoleur*," who puts things together in an ad hoc fashion from whatever materials are at hand.[7]

Read without looking through neo-Platonic glasses, Genesis seems closer to the Modoc story than to the Timaeus in that while surely we do not think of Yahweh as creating with a blank mind, nevertheless, neither are we to think that He has at His disposal eternal and perfectly intelligible forms for use in creating the world. He does not know, consequently, as does the Craftsman, what creation *must* be like. For Yahweh to know that He must look at it. Only after He has looked at it, that is, only after it is made, is He able to say, "It is good."

On the other hand, unlike Kumokums, Yahweh has more than idle curiosity and doodling hands.[8] He has serious and thoughtful intentions. His ideas are somewhat indeterminate, lacking the detail and precision of a blueprint, and they are the upsurge of His own creativity. While Yahweh's "Let there be" is a speech-act having the tone of political command, it is also a kind of oral poetry, sharing with ordinary speech an ultimately mysterious beginning. Just as a phenomenology of speaking shows that our words do not originate in transparency and light but emerge into consciousness from some dark and hidden region of our being and issue from our mouths to be heard for the first time by ourselves at the same time as they are heard by others, so Yahweh's creative words issue from what is a background, even for Him. In Genesis Yahweh is

phenomenology - self-awareness, consciousness

not portrayed as omniscient. Even His judgment about the good-ness of the creation appears to have been a bit hasty in the light of His subsequent decision to destroy much of it by flood.

As for Yahweh's use of raw materials, the issue is complex. The references in Genesis 1:2 to "waters" and an "abyss," along with the fact that "*bereshith*" (God's creative act) means "to cut out and put into shape," suggest a primordial chaos, and Philo of Alexandria gave a Timaeuslike account of creation, including the presence of preexistent matter. On the other hand, etymology is not a sure guide to authorial intent or sound interpretation. Virtu-ally all biblical prophets and many of the Psalms seem to assume God made everything, and the later orthodox doctrinal formula-tions favor a creation out of nothing. Unlike these later theologi-cal interpretations, the original story seems to be indifferent to all the issues surrounding matter. The situation is largely indetermi-nate. Nothing is said of its eternity or any inherent power to resist Yahweh's creative will; indeed, by contrast to the lengthy treat-ment of matter in *Timaeus*, Genesis mentions it only in passing. God's role in the story is all that is important.

The world that results from the P-account of creation is quite different from that of the Timaeus. First, the things of the created order are not composite. Form and matter did not exist eternally distinct until united by God but are primordially and inextricably integrated.[9] From the first they appear together in an ambiguous (ambiguous from the later perspective of Aristotelian logic) unity. This circumstance, along with the absence of preexistent, eternal, pure forms, means that the world is not fully intelligible. Because it is the product of God's autonomous will, it is contingent; in freedom God could have made a different world than He did. As His handiwork, the world, *including* its material aspect, is both good and real. Finally, the world is temporal. This follows from translating the opening phrase of the story, as a number of schol-ars have done, as "In the beginning of His creating, God made heaven and earth." Genesis depicts the getting underway of a process that is continuous.

Beyond that, the creation story leads logically into saga and even history proper. This implies that myth in Genesis reflects and contributes to the rise of historical consciousness in ancient Israel. It is an eschatological myth rather than a myth of eternal return and is, therefore, integrated with an ongoing history. This amounts to what John Priest calls the "reorientation of the locale

God's
world
good
real
contin-
gent
temporal

of myth" such that "for Israel history itself became the mode or vehicle of mythology."[10]

## TIMAEUS VERSUS GENESIS

Consider the way in which differences in any field of cultural endeavor quickly become crystallized into a very small number of competing options, most frequently two options in a relation of binary opposition. One thinks of eternity versus temporality, cosmos versus creation, space versus time, cyclical time versus linear time, to name a few. The twoness of this phenomenon has been explained in terms of the fact that humans have two hands or two hemispheres in the brain. While I am prepared to admit that our bodies do contribute to the shape of our knowledge, I cannot subscribe to a reductionism that finds a sufficient cause in anatomy or physiology. Certainly the content of these options is often, in my view, a partial function of the twin tributaries feeding Western civilization—namely, the myths of Timaeus and Genesis. In what follows I will try to demonstrate that contention. A few cautionary comments are, however, in order here.

First of all, I do not insist that all Greek and Hebraic ideas necessarily conflict with each other. Second, not all polar oppositions are Hebraic-Greek in nature. In this regard one has only to think of Nietzsche's distinction between Dionysian and Apollonian elements in Greek culture. Eternity versus temporality was an issue between Heraclitus, on the one hand, and Parmenides, on the other, an issue that resulted in Plato's metaphysical dualism of worlds. The ancient Hebrews, by contrast, abhorred dualisms, both social and intellectual, and either resolved or prevented them by radically embracing time.[11] Third, following the Alexandrian conquests the two cultures began to come into serious contact and at least by the time of Philo of Alexandria there arose a Timaeus-influenced interpretation of Genesis. By now there have been two millennia of interaction so that identifying what is Greek and what is Hebraic is as difficult as identifying what is a Japanese and what is an American automobile. All the same, I believe that even when a theory consists of a variety of elements, some Greek and some Hebraic, the cultural origins of these elements are often discernible. Fourth, when two theories are binary opposites, it will often turn out to be the Hebraic-Greek elements in them which account for the opposition. Fifth, my use of the heading "Timaeus versus Genesis" should not be read as meaning that the two myths themselves intended to oppose each other. That would only perpetuate the confusion that myths are primitive theories. It is the theories stemming from these myths which sometimes find themselves in conflict. Finally, what is important to understand here is that even when Hebraic-Greek oppositions emerge, the Hebraic position is framed not in its own terms but in Greek ones. This is because the intellectual standards governing serious discourse were based on Greek metaphysics, epistemology, and logic, that is to say, on the Timaeus. In the discussion that follows the reader should be able to recognize in the physiognomy of a theory its family resemblance to the Timaeus or Genesis and identify some of the genes from which that resemblance springs.

*Big Bang versus Steady State Cosmology*

In the 1920s astronomers began studying the spectra of light in stars belonging to galaxies other than our own. What they discovered is that although in most respects those spectra were like the ones found in our own galaxy, there was one significant difference—namely, as the examination of light moved to dimmer and dimmer images, the color shift along the spectrum moved toward the red end. This phenomenon, although interpretable in several ways, was understood, in accordance with the theory of the Doppler effect, to imply that the universe was not static, as had been previously believed, but was expanding. In other words, the galaxies were moving away from each other and doing so at a rate which is proportional to their distance.

Physicist George Gamow, among others, reasoned that if at present the galaxies are moving apart, then in the past they must have been closer together. The farther back in time one goes, the greater their proximity. Finally, at some time in the very remote past the matter that comprises the stars must have been crowded into a supercondensed state. Presumably, "in less time than it takes to cook a dish of duck and roast potatoes,"[12] the expansion of matter and the evolution of the universe began in what has become known as the "big bang." What, if anything, preceded and caused the supercondensed state and what triggered the explosion can never be known. This exceptional state of affairs, beyond which our minds, it is said, cannot penetrate, is called a "singularity." Here the density of the universe and the curvature of space-time would be infinite and, therefore, regarded as being beyond the scope of mathematics. Here, too, general relativity theory itself breaks down. Any events which did occur before the big bang would be useless for scientific purposes and might as well be ignored, leaving the universe with a beginning.

The principal rival to the big bang is the "steady state" theory of Hermann Bondi, Thomas Gold, and Frederick Hoyle. Rather than proceeding in a largely empiricist manner, these men adopted an a priori approach by assuming what Bondi called "the perfect cosmo-logical principle," from which the structure of the universe is deduced. It states that the general appearance of the universe as a whole would be the same no matter the place or time of the observation. Hoyle suggested that if a film were made of the galaxies moving away from us and finally disappearing from view, casual observers who dosed off during the showing of the film would notice virtually no change in the movie when they awakened. The reason is that as galaxies move beyond the horizon of our sight, new matter comes into being to form galaxies which replace the previous ones. If reversed, the film would never show a supercondensed state or big bang but the gradual dissolution of galaxies and the disappearance of the matter comprising them. The sameness of overall structure is maintained infinitely; there is no beginning or end to the universe. The new matter required of this theory appears at an average rate of "one atom in the course of a year in a volume equal to that of a moderate-sized skyscraper,"[13] a rate impossible to detect. Hoyle anticipates the obvious objection:

> Where does the created matter come from? It does not come from anywhere. Material simply appears—it is created. At one time the various atoms composing the material do not exist, and at a later time they do. This may seem a very strange idea and I do agree that it is, but in science it does not matter how strange an idea may seem so long as it works—that is to say, so long as the idea can be expressed in a precise form and so long as its consequences are found to be in agreement with observation.[14]

Not surprisingly, physicists, philosophers, and theologians noticed that the big bang, with its emphasis on a beginning and ending (when all the galaxies have moved beyond observation and the universe appears empty) and an evolution producing fundamental change, resembled Genesis. In 1951 the Roman Catholic church pronounced the big bang to be in harmony with the Bible. Physicist Stephen Hawking notes that it was this same recognition which prompted other scientists, put off that the big bang "smacks of divine intervention," to search for an alternative. These included "Russians because of their Marxist belief in scientific determinism and . . . people who felt that the whole idea of singularities was repugnant and spoiled the beauty of Einstein's theory."[15] Less recognized was that the steady state theory's emphasis on perfection, deduction, the absence of a beginning or ending, and insistence on a constant, unchanging pattern despite a flux of insignificant, particular changes owed much to the Timaeus. Hoyle himself, however, who used "Nature" in the title of his book in contrast to Gamow's "Creation," was cognizant of his dependency.

> The big bang theory requires a recent origin of the Universe that openly invites the concept of creation, while so-called thermodynamic theories of the origin of life in the organic soup of biology are the contemporary equivalent of the voice of the burning bush and the tablets of Moses.
> This is why I am unrepentantly Greek in my attitude to science. The Greeks believed there was an ultimate, discoverable order in the Universe whereas western religion holds that science can only go so far in explaining it.[16]

In my view, the consonance of the competing cosmological theories with Genesis and Timaeus is not a curious accident but a clue to the tacit reliance upon myth for the formulation of the theories in the first place. Here myth provides more than presuppositions about nature as good and real or about method—the ways in which myth was admitted to affect science by some of the thinkers discussed in Chapter 3—it also bears significantly on the content of scientific theories themselves. This takes myth into the very heart of science.

### Essentialism versus Existentialism: Anthropology

It would be a mistake to think that because the Timaeus and Genesis deal directly with cosmology that the reach of the two myths can be measured only on a cosmic scale. They also underlie a debate within philosophical anthropology. For my purposes, existentialist Jean-Paul Sartre's way of framing the problem in his "Existentialism is a Humanism" will suffice as an illustration.

Sartre says that the essentialist position can be summed up in the expression "essence precedes existence." This means that from birth all human beings are endowed with an essence or nature, that which makes anything what it is rather than something else. There are, for example, a variety of triangles; some are isosceles, some scalene, some equilateral. The length of their sides and the degree of their angles may differ. All triangles, however, no matter their size and shape, possess three sides and three interior angles whose sum is 180 degrees. This common possession is the nature of triangles; it is their essence. It is expressible in a definition. For an essentialist, everything, including human beings, has a definable essence like geometrical figures.

The essence of human beings, according to Aristotle and Thomas Aquinas, is their rationality. People are defined as "rational animals." A person is a member of a genus (animal) and a species (rational). What defines persons is not the way they differ from each other but what they share as members of a class. The class features are their nature or essence. The particular, unique features are regarded as incidental or as mere accidents. This essence is fixed from birth. Just as an acorn is destined from the beginning to become an oak tree, so human babies are destined to grow toward actualizing their potential for rationality. One can resist or fail to reach one's destiny but the result will be a life of unhappiness.

Essentialists do not, of course, fail to speak of existence, but it is understood merely as the power by which there are actual instances in the world of any essence. A unicorn, for example, has an essence, a certain nature, but it has no existence since there are no unicorns. Cows have both an essence and an existence.

Existentialists, on the other hand, view essentialism as stifling and oppressive. The slogan "existence precedes essence" insists that human beings are free, that they are not stuck at birth with a nature which limits them, constrains them, a nature about which they had no opinion or choice. It is not forced on them as an alien thing but is created during the course of life by the decisions they make, the acts they perform. Human essence is, therefore, historical rather than natural and is completed only at death. We alone determine what we are—not our bodies with their genetic codes, not rationality, not even God.

For existentialism, one's choices are always individual, unique, particular. This means that only as biological organisms and not as human beings are we members of a class. We can, of course, fail to exercise our freedom. We can conform uncritically to the crowd and thus surrender our humanity. To acquiesce to the crowd or to blame one's genes or environment is to live inauthentically, to have "bad faith." Our ultimate responsibility for our lives cannot be eradicated, however, since we are responsible even for the act of turning our lives over to another. We are, as Sartre put it, "condemned to be free."

Essentialism's debt to the Timaeus is patent. The notion of essence derives from Plato's Forms. That it is unchanging reflects the Forms' nontemporality. It's definability is a function of the pure intelligibility of the Forms and their use as models for the material world. The fact that human essence is constituted by class features rather than individual ones is due to the Forms' general or genuslike character.

The influence of Genesis on existentialism is equally obvious. Making will central to human personality and understanding it as free reflects the biblical view of both God and humankind as constituted by autonomous will. The historical character of existence follows readily from the historical character of creation itself in Genesis. Finally, the fundamental particularity of persons is consonant with a creating that made no use of generic forms but produced unique individuals.

## Phenomenology versus History of Religions: Methodology

As tales of travelers and reports of missionaries about non-Christian religions were supplemented by the translation of sacred texts and by fieldwork, scholarly examination of the other traditions began in earnest. The general approach to this study came to be known as "comparative religions." It consisted of adopting a set of categories, such as "God," "savior," "holy book," etc., in terms of which the individual religions were analyzed. Critics pointed out that Zen and Theravada Buddhism, for example, had no God. Even in the case of a religion like Islam, which could fill in the categorial blanks with "Allah," "Muhammad," and "Koran," there were problems. Both Muhammad and orthodox Islam claim that the prophet was nothing more than a human being who became the vehicle of a divine message. He was not a divine savior.

The realization grew that the categories were Christian in derivation and their use necessarily distorted one's view of the other religions and that a religion's inability to fill the categories might imply a negative assessment of its worth. The proper under-standing of any religion, scholars recognized, demanded an analysis on its own terms; consequently, a new method was in order.

The new method, designated "phenomenology of religion," sought to retain the idea of categories. They ensured the uniform, consistent treatment of all religions. They could not, however, be borrowed from any particular religion, otherwise the previous problems would persist. The categories must, instead, be universal in nature, derived by an intuition into the universal essence shared by all religions. Aztec sacrifice, Vedic sacrifice, and ancient Hebrew sacrifice, etc., could be seen as particular, local, culturally conditioned manifestations and illustrations of sacrifice in general and part of the essence of religion in general. Since the categories expressed the essence of all religions, they distorted none.[17] This genus-species typology is evidently a legacy of Aristotle's biology, which, in turn, is a modification and application of Plato's Forms, which find their connection to the material world in the Timaeus.

The phenomenology of religion itself, in turn, produced a critical reaction. It assumed at the outset of the investigation of the religions what could only be properly affirmed at its conclusion—namely, that a universal essence did exist. Such an approach was not sufficiently empirical. None of the semitic religions, with their belief that particulars are real and significant, would admit that "at bottom" all religions were the same. Moreover, some scholars pointed out that religious ideas and rituals arise out of particular historical circumstances and change over time as those circumstances themselves change. Obvious similarities may conceal a difference of meaning between Vedic sacrifice and Hebrew sacrifice or even between Vedic sacrifice in one era and Vedic sacrifice centuries later. The only proper solution to these difficulties is the study of each particular religion in the course of its historical development. Only at the conclusion of such a comprehensive task, which, because of the unavailability of sacred texts or their translation for some religions, might take generations, could sound judgments be made about a possible universal essence. This general approach, called the "history of religions,"[18] eventually reached an accommodation with phenomenology, whose meaning became altered.[19] In its insistence on particularity, uniqueness, and the historical character of religion, ideas rooted in Genesis, the Hebrew lineaments of the history of religions are clearly discernible.

### Covering Law versus Continuous Series Explanations: The Logic of Scientific Explanation

Earlier in this century one of philosophy's preoccupations was the logical analysis of language. Carl G. Hempel and Paul Oppenheim focused their attention on the logic of scientific explanation.[20] According to their "covering law" model, an explanation consists of an explanans (general laws and statements about initial conditions) and an explanandum (description of the empirical phenomenon to be explained). Because the two components are causally related, the latter can be logically deduced from the former. An explanation, then, has the following general form:

$C_1, C_2 \ldots\ldots\ldots C_k$    Statement of antecedent conditions
$L_1, L_2 \ldots\ldots\ldots L_r$    General Laws

___

E    Description of phenomenon to be explained

In addition, Hempel stated four "conditions of adequacy" for scientific explanations.

1. The explanandum must be actually deducible from the explanans.
2. The explanans must contain general laws and these must be necessary for the deduction.
3. The explanans must have consequences empirically testable in principle.
4. The explanans must be true.

These four conditions are necessary because the logical form of the explanation is not sufficient to rule out such unscientific explanations as the following:

Billy put a tooth under the pillow (initial conditions)
The tooth fairy always replaces teeth with money (law)

___

Thus Billy found a quarter beneath his pillow.

This "deductive-nomological" model and its deductive-statistical and inductive-statistical variations are alike in employing a law (deductive or inductive, nomological or statistical) to cover or subsume an event.

One of the most controversial features of the covering law

model was Hempel's claim of explanation-prediction symmetry. He said that an explanation and a prediction have the same logical form; the two are distinguished only by the pragmatic consideration of whether the "explanation" is given before the event to be explained or afterward. When critics Norwood Hanson and Michael Scriven gave counterexamples of predictions which were not explanations (Babylonian tide tables can predict but not explain tides, for example) and explanations which were not predictions (the behavior of a single beta particle, the collapse of a bridge), Adolf Grünbaum defended Hempel by arguing that such asymmetries are merely epistemological, not logical; the asymmetry resides in the "recordability of data" (whether the data is recorded before or after the event). Hempel himself acknowledged Scriven's contention that examination of a crucial, broken beam can explain after the fact why a bridge collapsed but that the collapse cannot be predicted in advance because such factors as load stresses, lightning discharges, wind velocities are not known. Hempel counters that while prediction may not be possible in practice, it is possible in principle (i.e., if we had the requisite knowledge).

Another of Scriven's criticisms is that sample explanations offered by Hempel omit many pieces of information which are essential to a strict logical deduction; that explanations are actually "explanation sketches," providing only such completeness as is necessary to produce understanding; and that in practice general laws function not to give explanations but to justify an explanation already given. Hempel replied that the incomplete explanations actually given necessarily presuppose fully explicit ones, hence most explanations are "elliptical" rather than sketchy. Elliptical explanations assume that explicit explanations have been or can be given.

Finally, May Brodbeck argues that objections to the deductive-nomological model, such as those made by Hanson and Scriven, presuppose a subjective view of explanation, one in which explanation is relative to particular persons and contexts. Such explanations, she argues, are merely psychological, not logical. Ewing Chinn concurs and says that the subject should be excluded from accounts of explanation by replacing the formula "X explains P to y" with the objective formula "P explains Q."[21]

The debate over the covering law model expanded when Hempel claimed that such explanations applied not only to science but also to history.[22] A legitimate explanation of Napoleon's defeat at Waterloo would not consist of an account in which the particular causes or reasons operative at Waterloo were narrated but an appeal to a law governing the behavior of military leaders or engagements of a certain general type. The principal critic of this move was William Dray, who believed that historiography was comprised of singular statements about particular persons and events. He set forth the continuous series model of explanation.[23] He asks us to imagine, for example, that an auto mechanic inquires of another mechanic what is wrong with a car that the latter is repairing. The second mechanic might reply, "It's got a leak in the oil pan." Such an explanation, although obviously very brief, would suffice. If the owner of the car, however, who is, presumably, a layperson in automobile mechanics, were to return and question the mechanic after having left the car for diagnosis, the abbreviated answer would not do. The mechanic would be required to reply somewhat as follows: "The oil reservoir near the middle of the car contains a supply of oil. Under the pressure of an oil pump the oil runs out of the reservoir into oil lines and moves forward toward the engine where it runs into the space between the walls of the pistons and the walls of the engine block, making the walls slippery and reducing friction as the pistons move up and down. When a hole developed in the oil reservoir of your car, then all the oil ran out through the hole onto the ground, leaving no oil for the pistons. The increase in friction in the engine block led to an increase in temperature to the point that the pistons were distorted in shape so badly that they could not move up and down any longer. Thus, the car stopped." While parts of the sequence could be put into covering law form, as Hempel pointed out, Dray countered that the laws are only sublaws covering the parts and not the events taken as a whole. The abbreviated explanation shared by the two mechanics works because they can take for granted, as the layperson cannot, the more comprehensive one. From this perspective, the covering law model was adequate neither to history nor science.

The ancestry of most features of the covering law model are traceable to the Timaeus. Insofar as a law states a general and stable pattern it recalls Plato's Forms which constitute a general and eternal pattern. That an explanation of empirical events subsumes them under a general law is homologous in structure to a material world which exists under and is made rational by a world of forms above it. The emphasis on form alone as providing an explanation coincides with Plato's notion that form alone is the object of knowledge. The deductive nature of the model in two of its versions is consonant with a necessary world made according to a fixed set of patterns. Explanation-prediction symmetry is precisely what one would expect from a myth in which time is unreal and cannot generate a future differing essentially from the past. The time of recordability of data is insignificant from the perspective of eternity. The distinctions between in practice and in principle, psychology and logic, epistemology and logic, and subjective and objective explanations are consequences of a view of knowledge as being universal like the Forms, which are its object. They make no concessions to a knower who has a body, a particular language, and a cultural context of understanding but presuppose a universal subject whose intellect is unaffected by its insertion into a body and a material-historical world. The covering law model amounts to a serious assault upon the narrative form as expressive of a certain mode of knowing.

Continuous series explanations, by contrast, model the temporal character of reality in Genesis. Indeed, as Arthur Danto and W. B. Gallie have pointed out, such an explanation is a narrative which tells the story of the interaction of several events.[24] The rejection of explanation-prediction symmetry is due to the belief that future history cannot be predicted in advance, not even by Yahweh. The "sketchy" character of explanations and their ultimate unspecifiability results from creation's contingent and not wholly intelligible character and it is an acknowledgement that what actually makes an event understandable will vary according to the individual knower.

### Myth versus History in Barthes': Structural Linguistics

Roland Barthes' *Mythologies* illustrates the clash between Genesis and the Timaeus within a single theoretical work. Starting from Ferdinand de Saussure's semiotics, Barthes offers an extended stipulative definition of myth as it exists today.

Myth, he says, cannot be defined by its content or substance; it is not a concept, idea, or an object. It is a "type of speech," "a system of communication," a "mode of signification."[25] More specifically, myth is a metalanguage in which one speaks about the first language.

Suppose, says Barthes, that I send a bouquet of roses to the person I love. On the "plane of experience" or the "plane of 'life'" there are only the unified, concrete "'passionified' roses." On the "plane of analysis," however, there is a "signifier" (the roses), the "signified" (my passion), and the "sign" (the signifier and signified as related by association). The sign is a first-order meaning on the "plane of language." "Language" is understood here to be any unit of meaning: a photograph, a drawing, an Inca *quipu*, or words.

This unit of meaning, however, can be "stolen" and "distorted," "deformed," or "consumed" by a metalanguage on the "plane of myth." Barthes offers the illustration of a photograph on the cover of a magazine of a "young Negro in a French uniform saluting" the *tricolour*. This Black soldier saluting is the first level of meaning. By an act of "larceny" that meaning becomes a new signifier (technically a "form") on the plane of myth. There it signifies, on an innocent reading, the glorious and color-blind French empire and, on a cynical reading, an alibi for French colonialist ambitions. This new signified, now on the plane of myth, is "the concept." Form and concept together constitute the "signification."

Clearly, mythic signification has political dimensions. It is precisely the function of myth to depoliticize the uses of meaning by "naturalizing" them—that is, turning them into eternal essences beyond question. Naturalization disguises the fact that myth is chosen, somewhat arbitrarily, by history from among a variety of options that were available. Myth, then, is a tool by which the bourgeoisie keeps at bay the Revolution. The bourgeoisie wish to maintain a status quo in which their power is secured. Revolutionary politics, by contrast, which seeks transformation, is inherently antimythical. It regards the state of affairs as still up for grabs. Myth sides with immobility and tries to stop the "ceaseless making" of the world and acts as "a prohibition for man against inventing himself."

The presence of the Timaeus is particularly clear here. The double set of planes (experience or life, on the one hand, and analysis, language and myth, on the other) reflect Plato's intelligible and material planes or worlds. That meaning is unified on the plane of experience but separated on the plane of analysis parallels the unity of form and matter in the manufactured object, on the one hand, and the separated Form and matter with which the Craftsman worked, on the other. Association, the relation by which the signifier and the signified are united in the sign (on the plane of language) and by which form and concept are united in the signification (on the plane of myth), is an external relationship as is the relationship of Form, matter, and Craftsman in the Timaeus. Analysis provides understanding by reversing manufacture; it dissolves the artificial unity and returns the resulting elements to their original, dissociated state wherein is perfect clarity. Myth's aim to immobilize, naturalize, and essentialize history remains true to Plato's aim to provide a static and eternal anchor against the ravages of flux and time.

Genesis, on the other hand, appears in Barthes' approval of a Marxist revolution, as well as in his emphasis on the historical nature of reality, the inventedness of human existence, and the transformative power of choice. Marxism's debt to the Bible is well-documented and widely recognized.

The number of rival theories generated by the Timaeus and Genesis is hardly exhausted by the preceding discussion. The list of illustrations could be expanded considerably. Nor is this clash of myths confined to the twentieth century. Earlier manifestations of it include the following debates: immortality of the soul versus resurrection of the body, fate versus hope, nominalism versus realism, voluntarism versus intellectualism, faith versus reason, empiricism versus rationalism, and uniformitarianism versus catastrophism. Structuralism's distinction between synchronic and diachronic relations also reflects the two myths.

It is important to reiterate, however, the way in which, in most instances, the Hebraic side of the opposition is framed by Greek ways of thinking. For example, the Greeks had no concept of will, only reason and desire. What passed for will was the hybrid notion of reasonable desire or desireful reason. The Bible, by contrast, portrays humans and Yahweh as beings who decide and act. Will is a much more determinate notion in which Greek thinking turned decision and action into a rational faculty of more limited scope, which was often in conflict with intellect. The empiricism of the early modern period also had such Greek elements as sense data (a Democritean and Newtonian atomism of the mind) and a Pythagorean emphasis on the measurable features of the phenomenal world (primary qualities).[26] Both uniformitarianism and catastrophism in geology are a tangle of Greek and Hebraic elements.

## THE TACIT DIMENSION

Readers convinced of the striking and frequent homologies between Genesis and the Timaeus, on the one hand, and modern theoretical structures, on the other, may, nevertheless, have questions about the way in which ancient myths could exert influence on contemporary intellectual discourse. Some of the answers must be postponed until the next chapter; however, others can be supplied here. My contention is that these myths are not confined to a distant past, affecting the present by means of a series of intermediate historical causes; instead, they are alive in the present and exercise their authority directly. How this is so will be explained with the help of philosopher-scientist Michael Polanyi.

Although Polanyi sets out to articulate a theory of scientific discovery, his conclusions apply equally well to other forms of theoretical knowledge. His principal claim is that scientific knowing cannot be achieved by explicit inferences, deductive or inductive, but relies from start to finish on the tacit powers of the mind and its content. His insistence upon the omnipresence of a tacit coefficient in all acts of knowing and perceiving defines his "post-critical" epistemology.

For a logic of tacit knowing suitable to his purposes, Polanyi turns to perception as studied by Gestalt psychologists. He offers an example of tacit knowing in the perception of a moving hand.

> When I move my hand before my eyes, it would keep changing its colour, it shape and its size, but for the fact that I take into account a host of rapidly changing clues, some in the field of vision, some in my eye muscles and some deeper still in my body, as in the labyrinth of the inner ear. My powers of perceiving coherence make me see these thousand varied and changing clues jointly as one single unchanging object, as an object moving about at different distances, seen from different angles, under variable illumination. A successful integration of a thousand changing particulars into a single constant sight makes me recognise a real object in front of me.[27]

Two kinds of awareness are involved in this act of perception: a subsidiary awareness of the clues and a focal awareness of their joint meaning or object. Attending subsidiarily *from* the clues *to* their focal meaning is a skillful act, however routine, which has a vectorial or directed character.

The subsidiary-focal and tacit-explicit distinctions are relative ones; they do not constitute new dichotomies. Just as in visual perception there is no sharp line separating focal from peripheral perception, what is explicit or focal, in any feat of knowing or perceiving, shades gradually into the tacit or subsidiary. Moreover, what is tacit-subsidiary in one moment may be shifted to the explicit-focal in the next, although there are some tacit-subsidiary clues which can never be made explicit-focal.

Confirmation of tacit knowing comes in the form of scientific studies in subception. Persons exposed to brief presentations of nonsense syllables, certain of which were followed by electric shocks, were soon able to anticipate the shocks but could not say how they were able to do so. This illustrates Polanyi's claim that we can know more than we can say. Whenever we attend focally to what, moments before, were tacit or "marginal" clues, however, the clues undergo a modification of form as a result of becoming explicit; they become more determinate. Thus, their contribution to any focal or explicit meaning cannot be fully specified. Moreover, other clues cannot be made explicit ("subliminal" clues). This tacit dimension is not merely a contingent psychological fact which may be ignored but is a logical and necessary fact, one from which, not even in principle, is there an escape.[28]

Tacit knowing is rooted in the body, which, grasped phenomenologically, is a "system" of tacit powers. The body, according to Polanyi, can extend itself by a process of "indwelling" or "interiorizing" as when one uses a hammer. The pressures of the hammer's handle on the hand are interiorized and become tacit clues directing the swing of the hammer's head toward the nail, the object of focal awareness. On the other hand, shifting focal awareness to the previously tacit clues becomes a process of "alienation" or "exteriorization," which destroys the whole the clues comprised. Pianists, for example, who attend focally from the music to the individual movements of their fingers become "all fingers" and the music suffers or stops altogether. Our most important "tool" is language, whose effective use is largely a matter of tacit knowing.

In the realm of science the routine skills of perception are augmented by reflection and imagination in the service of scientific discovery. Here the tacit dimension becomes a matter of "connoisseurship" developed during an apprenticeship in a specialized community under the direction of a veteran scientist. The range of tacit clues required for such acts as making sophisticated scientific measurements, picking out promising lines of inquiry, or formulating scientific theories is also vastly expanded. The logic of knowing involved in scientific discovery, however, differs only in "range and degree" from the tacit knowing exhibited in perception; both require the reliance upon an integration of tacit clues in order to attend focally to their joint meaning.

The tacit dimension, however, operates even more broadly than in science alone. For all forms of reflection the tacit dimension includes presuppositions which constitute an "interpretive framework" which we "assimilate" and with which we "identify."[29]

Polanyi's logic of tacit knowing offers the possibility of handling several objections the reader may have begun to entertain and also of outlining a radically different understanding of the functioning of myth, especially in the modern context. All of these possibilities rest on the claim that first and foremost myth belongs to the tacit dimension, that the presuppositions and interpretive framework of which Polanyi speaks are derived from myth, which lies or functions even more deeply in the tacit dimension.

In claiming that the Timaeus myth, for example, has been and is generative of much of Western culture I am not claiming that *Timaeus* is a widely read work. Most people educated in a liberal arts tradition will, however, have heard in a philosophy, classics, humanities, or Western civilization class the story of Timaeus. Thereafter, the story, or images derived from it, may function as part of their tacit framework. Even persons who have never encountered the Timaeus in any explicit form may be dependent on it by extension in the sense that they indwell and tacitly rely on ontologies, epistemologies, or methodologies stemming from it.

Nor am I denying that all the theoretical positions treated in the previous section can be derived, without any explicit reference to myth, from either the philosophies of Plato and Aristotle or Jewish and Christian theology. I would simply counter that these more determinate philosophical and theological doctrines are themselves derived from Genesis, Timaeus, and other myths of their respective cultural traditions.

One could object, however, that Plato's philosophical views (the Forms, for example) cannot be derived from the Timaeus because *Timaeus* was not written until very late in his life, well after *The Republic* and other dialogues in which the forms appear. While a final answer to this objection must await the next chapter, some things can be said here.

First, it is possible that early on Plato relied on the Timaeus story in his philosophizing but chose to put it down in writing only at the end of his career. In the absence of any evidence to that effect, however, this argument from silence does little to settle the issue. It does seem quite probable to me that Plato relied from the outset, at least tacitly, on the earlier and simpler stories of Prometheus and Daedalus, whose technological and engineering orientation received a more complicated reworking in *Timaeus*. It may be worth noting that the P-account of creation in the Bible was also written quite late in the formation of the Pentateuch and relied, in part, on the reworking of previously extant Meso-potamian myths. In anticipation of the next chapter I can add that even if the Timaeus were not conceived or articulated until late in Plato's career, he was surely guided in his theoretical endeavors by his tacit awareness of a prereflective form of life to which the Timaeus would subsequently give verbal expression.

Earlier on, I acknowledged that the theories considered in the previous section could be derived from theological and philosoph-ical doctrines rather than myths; nevertheless, the reader will have already discerned from the discussion following that acknowledg-ment that even if such a derivation did occur, I do not believe that is the whole story. One reason for this view is found in Ian Bar-bour's treatment of the role of theoretical models in the extension of theories. What he claims for models I would also claim for myths. Metaphors, he argues, posit analogies between entities or events. Models are systematically developed metaphors. In sup-port of his view that the extension of theories comes from models rather than other theories Barbour quotes Mary Hesse:

> The theoretical model carries with it what has been called 'open texture' or 'surplus meaning', derived from the familiar system. The theoretical model conveys associations and implications that are not completely specifiable and that may be transferred by analogy to the explanandum (the phenomenon to be explained); further developments and modifications of the explanatory theory may therefore be suggested by the theoreti-cal model. Because the theoretical model is richer than the explanandum, it imports concepts and conceptual relations not present in the empirical data alone.[30]

Barbour goes on to expand the claim:

> A model is grasped as a whole; it gives in vivid form a summary of complex relationships. It is said to offer 'epistemological

immediacy' or 'direct presentation of meaning'. Because of its vividness and intelligibility it is frequently used for teaching purposes to help a student understand a theory. *But even at the critical stages of discovery itself,* scientists report that visual imagery often predominates over verbal or mathematical thinking. . . . [31] (emphasis mine)

The same vividness, openness, and suggestiveness, etc., I contend, are characteristic of myths; consequently, it is reasonable in the light of Polanyi's model of tacit knowing to conclude that in both the original formulation and subsequent modification of theories myths are tacitly animating the imaginative and creative processes underlying those reflections.

Finally, in light of the foregoing it becomes possible to grasp in preliminary fashion the understanding that, as part of the tacit background, myths as such are neither ideological rivals nor primitive versions of theories, doctrines, laws, or any other explicit forms of intellectual achievement. On the contrary, they are part of the wherewithal, the clues, the "instruments" thinkers/actors tacitly rely on in every field of reflection/endeavor. We think *with* myths, even when myths themselves are what we think about.

The way in which myth functions in the process of thinking rather than as the object of thinking is perhaps illuminated by Spanish philosopher, Ortega y Gasset, who says:

My thinking already starts out with certain definite ideas, certain basic convictions, the outcome of all intellectual efforts made by past generations up to the time in which I begin to think. Being the deepest stratum of my subjectivity, those basic convictions form the mental groundwork from which my own quest takes off. This groundwork of my intellectual personality partakes of the diffuse collective life that is the human species up to the present moment. The intellect of the individual is not individual in the sense that it is free to forge its ideas from naught; it is, from the outset, shaped by the heritage of the historical collectivity. That which does the thinking in me is, in this perfectly empirical and by no means mystic sense, not merely I but also the whole human past.[32]

This past, which is continuously collected into a present-tacitly-shaping-reflection, includes myth. Indeed, myth is the more foundational and narrative part of the tacit dimension from which other and nonnarrative elements are derived.

## TIMAEUS VERSUS GENESIS IN HISTORICAL PERSPECTIVE

Modernity, then, is not mythless; rather, it is under the spell of multiple myths. The crisis of myth is a direct consequence not of the death or absence of myth but of a surplus of myths—that is, the fact that Western civilization continues to draw upon both its Hebraic and its Greek roots, both Genesis and the Timaeus. Like wrestlers in a ring, they roll and tumble about, first one on top, then the other. When Christianity appeared in Hellenistic culture, the two myths began a serious engagement in the work of Philo, Justin Martyr, and Origen, etc. Key to this engagement was relocating Plato's Forms inside the mind of God. The usual view that the Forms were removed from the context of Platonic philosophy and surgically inserted into the mind of Yahweh gives too much weight, in my view, to Genesis. Given the outcome of the process, it seems more likely that the Forms were placed inside a beefed-up Craftsman, who was hastily baptized as the biblical God. This sleight of texts was possible not only because of the relatively undeveloped state of biblical studies at the time but also because Genesis contains two accounts of creation, a fact unremarked at the time. The differences between the Timaeus and the P-account of creation are stark; however, there is an obvious superficial similarity between the Craftsman who molds matter in the shape of forms and the J-account's potter who shapes clay. That the biblical potter does not have preexistent and eternal forms, an absolutely crucial difference, is overlooked. Round one goes to the Timaeus. In Augustine's authoritative pronouncement that God and the drama of salvation alone should be the subject of theology Hebraic culture seized control of the content of Western thought, pushing nature aside. For its part, Greek culture seized control of the conceptual framework and intellectual standards in terms of which the themes of Christendom would be formulated. There was no clear victory, only a standoff. Later, with the recovery of Aristotle's texts from the Arabs, momentum shifted in favor of the Greeks. William Placher asserts that these texts "had an impact reminiscent of those science fiction stories in which the world suddenly encounters a civilization far in advance of its own."[33] The condemnations in 1277 by Etienne Tempier, Bishop of Paris, and Robert Kilwardby, Archbishop of Canterbury, of Greek-based philosophical propositions turned the tide once more toward Genesis. Francis Oakley calls this event "the overt starting point of a new tradition" and cites Étienne Gilson's statement that it marks the end of the honeymoon between philosophy and theology.[34] Soon the Reformation would call reason a whore, urge the ouster of Aristotle, and proclaim Scripture the sole religious authority. To the south, on the other hand, the Italian Renaissance gives the Greek heritage new momentum. The neo-Pythagorean revival, already described in Chapter 2, makes nature rather than God and salvation the principal object of study and gradually science becomes the dominant cultural force, before which theology and even philosophy have had to retreat. The Timaeus appears to have vanquished its rival.

If Genesis no longer seemed able to determine the content of cultural interest, as it had during the Augustinian era, it began, perhaps for the first time, to make itself felt in terms of shaping intellectual standards. Interestingly, this influence came in science itself. In the eighteenth century Lyell's *Principles of Geology* was significant in portraying the earth as historical in nature and in introducing the use of narrative to scientific writing. In the nineteenth, Darwin's theory of biological evolution, in doing for biology what Lyell had done for geology, brought scientific thinking in important respects closer to a biblical perspective, an irony entirely lost on his fundamentalist despisers. When such philosophers as Ernst Haeckel and Herbert Spencer, among others, elaborated evolution into a comprehensive narrative of all reality, fundamentalists saw something sufficiently resembling, and therefore threatening to, biblical myth. In this century it is physics which has undergone a revolution, undermining—although not everyone has yet received the news—the determinism, reductionism, and strict objectivity stemming from the Timaeus. Also, one way to read Deconstructionism, with its assaults on the metaphysics and epistemology of presence, is as trying to deliver, in the name of Genesis, by which it is partially and unwittingly motivated, the coup de grace to the Timaeus's long-standing control of reflection and its domination of modernity. Finally, it can be no accident that the three books mentioned at the outset of this chapter, all of which demonstrate the presence of myth in philosophy, that discipline in which Greek-based intellectual standards and controls are set forth, are historical. Indeed, history is a discipline with obvious links to Hebraic modes of understanding.

Such considerations lead back to the problems, described in Chapter 2, which modernity poses for understanding myth. The perspectives acquired in this and the previous chapters have prepared the way for my attempt in Chapter 5 to give those problems a novel and satisfactory resolution. There I will talk about ways of overcoming the inner-outer dichotomy and set forth a definition of "myth" which does not depend upon that dualism or the features of modernity that spring from it.

# CHAPTER 5

# Toward a Postcritical Understanding of Myth

I do not think I believe in lines. Look as I might, I can find them
nowhere save in constructions of the mind.
— Lindsay Clarke, *The Chymical Wedding*

At the end of Chapter 2 we saw that modern theories of myth
exhibit their authors' commitment to an ontology (and often an
epistemology based on it) whose origins were traced to the rise of
modern science. The result, even among those thinkers who
sought to defend myth from its detractors, was a reductionistic or
culturally schizophrenic understanding of myth and reality. Myth
was and is regarded by most interpreters, consequently, as associated with the primitive, the past, the subjective, or the false. Such
judgments assume, of course, that modernity itself, or some isolated and sophisticated part of it, has outdistanced myth and can
speak from a privileged, myth-free standpoint. Chapter 3 and
especially Chapter 4 challenged that assumption. Now that the
pervasiveness of myth has been demonstrated, I wish to take up
again the problem encountered in Chapter 2. Following Susanne
Langer, I took the dichotomy between inner experience and outer
world to be the defining feature of modernity. If this dualism is
found to be untenable, then the way is clear to seek an understanding of myth which moves beyond modernity.

For help in overcoming the inner-outer dichotomy I will look
to twentieth-century physics and existential phenomenology, especially that of Maurice Merleau-Ponty. Then I will lay out my own
theory of myth, one which is not based on an ontological or epistemological dualism. In due course, my own fundamental dependence upon Genesis will become evident and, consequently, force
the issue of the truth of myth. Finally, I will indicate how, within

the framework of a finite model of knowledge, to assess the truth of Genesis and the Timaeus.

## CONTEMPORARY PHYSICS AND CARTESIAN DUALISM

The dualism that defines modernity is based, as we saw in Chapter 2, on assumptions derived from early modern science. If we are to move beyond modernity in more than name only, we must come to understand the way in which twentieth-century physics has overthrown certain neo-Pythagorean notions common to Kepler, Galileo, and Descartes.

What English physicist Paul Davies wrote in 1983 is still true.

> Over fifty years ago something strange happened in physical science. Bizarre and stunning new ideas about space and time, mind and matter, erupted from the scientific community. Only now are these ideas beginning to reach the general public. . . . The fruits of this revolution are only now starting to be plucked by philosophers and theologians.[1]

Lack of acquaintance with the significance of these events and their philosophical implications extends, apparently, to those thinkers most highly critical of modernity. According to Terry Eagleton,

> The model of science frequently derided by poststructuralism is usually a positivist one—some version of the nineteenth-century rationalistic claim to a transcendental, value-free knowledge of 'the facts'.[2]

Let us examine briefly a few of the ways contemporary science undoes some neo-Pythagorean assumptions, especially the pivotal distinction between primary and secondary qualities.

### The Wave-Particle Dualism and Scientific Representation

Prior to this century such objects as electrons, baseballs, and planets (the microscopic, mesoscopic, and macroscopic) were regarded as particles, "a small lump of concentrated stuff," while water and light were regarded as waves, "an amorphous disturbance that can spread out and dissipate."[3] The properties defining waves and particles were mutually exclusive. In this century, however, it has been demonstrated that in some experimental situations light exhibits particlelike behavior. This occurs, for example, when photons, quantum units of light, are fired at a metal plate, knocking electrons out of the plate's back side (the "photoelectric effect"). On the other hand, electrons sometimes exhibit wavelike behavior. This happens when they are fired at a plate having two slits in it. The electrons pass through one or the other of the slits, making wavelike "interference" patterns on a photographic plate behind the first. Electrons and photons, then, along with other subatomic entities behave in apparently contradictory ways, upsetting the logic which neatly distinguishes waves from particles. In these and other ways subatomic reality has proven to be too bizarre, too ambiguous, too rich to be pictured adequately by either "wave" or "particle" alone. Many interpreters now view waves and particles as metaphors which have been elaborated into models related to each other by Niels Bohr's "Complementarity" principle—that is, each model supplies only a partial description of reality and the most adequate description requires both.

## The Uncertainty Principle

In quantum theory pairs of variables are related to each other in such a way that if an experimental situation is arranged to measure one of them precisely, the less precisely the other one can be measured. For example, if one wishes to determine with as much certainty as possible the position of an electron just after it has passed through one of the slits in the plate described above, there follows a corresponding loss of certainty about its lateral velocity, and vice versa. Position and velocity, however, were singled out by Kepler and Galileo as primary qualities—that is, qualities which are not projected by the mind onto nature but which are intrinsic features of material reality itself. Descartes translated and elaborated this distinction between primary and secondary qualities into his metaphysical distinction between *res extensa* (extended things or substances) and *res cogitans* (thinking substances), the ontological foundation of the dichotomy between inner experience and outer world. Now that position and velocity, primary qualities essential to the formulation of Newton's laws of motion, of his view of nature as a mechanism, and to scientific measurement and description, are not easily measurable and are characterized by an indeterminacy regarded by most scientists as inherent in nature, the inner-outer distinction is deprived of its scientific foundation.

*Goedel's Proof*

In his paper "On Formally Undecidable Propositions of Principia Mathematica and Related Systems" Kurt Goedel has shown that in any formal system one can construct formulae or sentences which are demonstrably undecidable within that system. An example is the sentence S, which says that any statement with the variable V in it is not provable. Sentence S, of course, is just such a sentence since it contains the variable V. So, if the statement is true, it is undecidable, or, if it is decidable, then it is untrue. Tarski has shown that the truth of S can be asserted, however, in a richer language than that comprising the formalized axioms of the system. This richer language is unformalized in terms of the formalized system.

The significance of the foregoing discussion comes into view by recalling that Galileo, the neo-Pythagorean, saw God as a geometer, His creation as a work of geometry, and mathematics as the one kind of human knowledge equal in certainty and truth to God's divine and omniscient knowledge. If it can be argued that indeterminacy amounts to the denial of an ontology of the world as mathematical (except in a statistical sense), then Goedel's proof can be viewed as a rejection of mathematics as the paradigm of perfect knowledge, the symbol of hope for utter clarity, precision, and certainty in all fields of knowledge—in other words, Descartes' dream of a *mathesis universalis.*

Finally, according to Ian Barbour, the wave-particle dualism implies the "loss of picturability"[4] by everyday concepts of subatomic entities. Moreover, since whether the wave or the particle properties appear and whether position or velocity is measurable depends upon human choice, the claims of strict objectivity for scientific theories about nature become problematic. The wider epistemological significance of these considerations, Barbour argues, is the rejection of naive realism, the view that our conceptions supply "concrete and exhaustive" descriptions of reality, in favor of "critical realism," in which they are regarded as "abstract and selective."[5] Thus, the inner-outer dichotomy is not being overcome, as Lévi-Strauss claims (see Chapter 2), by science's transformation of the subjective into the objective but by a partial subjectivization of science such that the distinction between the objective and the subjective becomes blurred.

Many physicists would contend that if subatomic entities are not describable in such everyday concepts as waves and particles, they are, nevertheless, describable in mathematical terms. Physicist David Finkelstein objects, however, that mathematical symbols, like all symbols, follow their own rules rather than following experience. Hence, a mathematical analysis of electrons, for example, is not better qualitatively than any other. He says, "The best you get with symbols is a maximal but incomplete description."[6]

Taken together, then, these and other revolutionary notions in twentieth-century physics subvert the ontological and epistemological foundations of modernity by rejecting the distinction between primary and secondary qualities and the inner-outer dichotomy built upon it.

## THE PHENOMENOLOGICAL TURN

Still another avenue for circumventing modernity's ontological and epistemological dualism runs through the phenomenological tradition founded by Edmund Husserl. Central to the movement is "intentionality," a concept Husserl borrowed from Franz Brentano and modified.[7] "Intentionality" is a way of characterizing consciousness. To say that consciousness is intentional is to deny that it consists of representations or ideas and to affirm that it is a directedness toward an object. As a direction, consciousness does not construct its object but discloses or displays it. While for Brentano the objects of consciousness were immanent in it, for Husserl they were present to it. The intentionality of consciousness was the basis for the radical and descriptive empiricism of Husserl's earliest phenomenological work, *Logical Investigations*, and in itself amounts to a serious blow to the distinction of inner and outer. It amounts not so much to a solution of the mind-body problem as to an announcement that the problem is ultimately a pseudoproblem. Consciousness and its object do not exist separately and are then, subsequently, brought into relationship with each other (as are form and matter in the Timaeus) but are primordially and constitutively together (as are form and matter in the P-account of Genesis).

After moving through a middle or idealistic stage, Husserl, in his final or existential stage, introduced the concept *Lebenswelt* or life-world. For Husserl, the life-world is an oriented, lived world preceding and underlying reflection. It is the encompassing context or frame of reference or "horizon" in which all things make

SEE p. 68

sense, insofar as they do. It is more fluid, more dynamic, more ambiguous than the picture of the world produced from it by abstract thinking. The life-world became the basis for the existentialist theories of Sartre, Heidegger, and Merleau-Ponty. Sartre, however, reduces the self to a nothingness pitted against the world (being). Heidegger, on the other hand, although he speaks of "being-in-the-world," is interested in an analysis of the being of the subject. His early work is a kind of existential noetics—that is, a focus on the subject pole of intentionality.

Merleau-Ponty, by contrast, states as early as the Preface of his *Phenomenology of Perception* that "truth does not 'inhabit' only 'the inner man', or more accurately, there is no inner man, man is in the world, and only in the world does he know himself."[8] For him, both subject and object are abstractions from the more primordial being-in-the-world, a phenomenon intimately related to Merleau-Ponty's most significant discovery—namely, the "body-subject." The body-subject is the key, in Merleau-Ponty's phenomenology to overcoming the dichotomy of inner and outer.

For both science and the philosophical tradition built on it, the body is defined as an object in Euclidian space. Science, however, is the "second-order expression" of an experienced and lived world about which it speaks and in relation to which "every scientific schematization is an abstract and derivative sign-language."[9] The fuller, more concrete, experienced body is a subject characterized by intentionality. Taking advantage of a distinction drawn by the later Husserl, Merleau-Ponty observes that the intentionality of the body as subject is not the "active intentionality" of judgment, reflection, or consciousness but the "operative intentionality" of the body as a prereflective, preconscious, system of "anonymous" powers. Whereas active intentionality intends or is directed toward an object, operative intentionality intends or is directed toward a world. Whereas the relation of the reflective subject to its object is epistemological, the relation of the body-subject to its world is also ontological. The boundaries of the self are opened up so that the subject both interacts with and *is* his or her body and world. Thus, Merleau-Ponty, who was a psychologist as well as a philosopher, speaks of a "motor intentionality," a "perceptual intentionality," and an "affective intentionality" to indicate the prereflective orientation and directionality in the body-subject's moving, perceiving, and feeling as it interacts intimately with the situation in which it finds itself and which it is.

The world is not only a natural one but also a social one. The other is known as my body perceives the other's body and grasps immediately the intentions of the other manifested through it. The human other is known most especially in language, not the abstract system of signs and signifiers of semioticians but in concrete acts of speaking which body forth a meaning emerging from a gestural sense. Speech is primarily a dialogue between body-subjects in which their coexistence and joint intention to communicate call forth speech anonymously the way my arm is called forth to swat a mosquito or scratch an itch. Just as it is unnecessary for me to locate where my arm is in objective space and reflectively direct its trajectory toward a consciously entertained target, so words are *with* me, have meaning as part of my body, and are launched into speech by an operative intentionality as one of the modalities of the body-subject's being-in-the-world. Impelled toward nature and society by motor intentionality and engaging them in an intimate coexistence by means of perceptual intentionality, affective intentionality, and the intentionality of speech, a world emerges, a world which "is always 'already there' before reflection begins—as an inalienable presence."[10]

If the Cartesian body is modified by Merleau-Ponty to make it into an anonymous subject, the mind is also reshaped to make it more bodily. Just as perception is the common meeting ground of science (the objective) and philosophy (the subjective), so speech is the place of meeting for mind and body. Mind is bodily because thought is embodied in language and language is rooted in bodily acts of speaking. Thought may begin in perception or feeling but it "tends toward expression as its completion." The "authentic speech," which formulates meaning for the first time, " . . . does not translate ready-made thought, but accomplishes it." Even when one reflects in silence, "this supposed silence is alive with words, this inner life is an inner language." Thus, says Merleau-Ponty,

> Thought and expression, then, are simultaneously constituted, when our cultural store is put at the service of this unknown law, as our body suddenly lends itself to some new gesture in the formation of habit. The spoken word is a genuine gesture, and it contains its meaning the same way as the gesture contains its.[11]

With the mind made bodily by speech and the body made into a subject by an operative intentionality directed toward a world, the integration of mind, body and world, already foreshadowed in "intentionality," is displayed.

If meaning is generated in acts of speaking performed by the body understood as a subject, then speaking, meaning, and language are a kind of doing. This perspective opens up solutions to problems raised by structuralist and poststructuralist theories of language. In commenting on the "undecidability" of language in Derrida's thought, Terry Eagleton says:

> Meaning may well be ultimately undecidable if we view language contemplatively, as a chain of signifiers on a page; it becomes 'decidable', and words like 'truth', 'reality', 'knowledge', and 'certainty' have some of their force restored to them, when we think of language rather as something we *do*, as indissociably interwoven with our practical forms of life. It is not of course that language becomes fixed and luminous: on the contrary, it becomes even more fraught and conflictual than the most 'deconstructed' literary text. It is just that we are then able to see, in a practical rather than academicist way, what would *count* as deciding, determining, persuading, certainty, being truthful, falsifying and the rest—and see, moreover, what beyond language itself is *involved* in such definitions.[12]

Merleau-Ponty would add that the academicist view is parasitically dependent upon those "practical" forms of life of which reflection is an intermittent modulation. Meaning is decided by the body-subject, which always plays the role of advance man for reflection's arrival. This explains how the visiting scholar, who gives a brilliant lecture on the undecidability of language is, nevertheless, unproblematically able, once the lecture is completed, to choose, in consultation with his or her hosts, a suitable restaurant, arrange for a taxi to take him there, order from the menu written in a foreign language, and understand both praise and criticism of the lecture offered by his dinner companions.

Merleau-Ponty's prereflective, anonymous body-subject also solves problems relating to perception. Stephen Daniel argued that even sense perception is determined by linguistic constructions. Such a claim reflects the assimilation of perception to thought effected by Descartes in order to ensure certainty. If one cannot be sure of the pain in one's foot, one can at least be sure, Descartes said, about the *thought* that one feels pain in one's foot. Perception became thought about perception. Thus, Daniel would agree, presumably, with Norwood Hanson, who, at the outset of his *Patterns of Discovery*, imagined Tycho Brahe, a believer in Ptolemaic cosmology, and Kepler, a Copernican, standing on a hill at dawn.

> Tycho sees the sun beginning its journey from horizon to horizon. He sees that from some celestial vantage point the sun . . . could be watched circling our fixed earth. Watching the sun at dawn through Tychonic spectacles would be to see it in something like this way.
>
> Kepler's visual field, however, has a different conceptual organization. Yet a drawing of what he sees at dawn could be a drawing of exactly what Tycho saw, and could be recognized as such by Tycho. But Kepler will see the horizon dipping, or turning away, from our fixed local star. The shift from sunrise to horizon-turn is analogous to the shift-of-aspect phenomena already considered; it is occasioned by differences between what Tycho and Kepler think they know.[13]

Hanson believes the two men *see* different worlds, as if acts of sensory perception were performed by minds or conceptualizations. In perceiving, however, the body-subject does not theorize. Planted on the hilltop in its facticity, in its spatial and temporal thickness, the body-subject offers no view from nowhere but anchors perception to and opens up the world from a particular spot. Thus, both men *see* the sun rise from the earth. Aided by Copernicus's theory, however, Kepler *thinks* that in this case perception is misleading. Like most thinkers since Descartes, Hanson confuses perceptual synthesis with that of intellectual judgment.

Inherence in a body makes Merleau-Ponty's subject and the knowledge of which the subject is capable finite. In that respect Merleau-Ponty and Polanyi are in agreement. Indeed, Polanyi came to see his view of knowing as embodied reliance upon tacit clues in order to attend focally to their joint meaning as consonant with Merleau-Ponty's elaborated notion of intentionality.[14] For both, the status and shape of thinking had to be reconsidered in order to reflect its clay feet. For Polanyi, that led to a conception of "personal knowledge." Merleau-Ponty spoke of a "radical reflection" which acknowledged its rootedness in a prereflective and existential dialectic of body and world. Reflection, of course, can make occasional corrections to the meanings arising from the life-world, but it cannot coherently abolish that world. In doing that reflection would cut off the limb on which it necessarily stands. In other words, both philosophers proposed, against the inherited intellectual tradition, a finite anthropology and a finite model of knowledge.

The abolition of the metaphysical dualism of inner and outer, the acquisition of an anthropology and epistemology of finitude, and an appreciation of the way myth is present in even our most sophisticated forms of thinking have now brought to completion the preparations for adumbrating a postcritical understanding of myth.

## THE NATURE OF MYTH

My aim here is not, as was Doty's, to attempt a comprehensive treatment of myth but to concentrate upon the ways in which my view of myth goes beyond those of modernity. I shall, however, follow Doty's example of laying out a theory by means of an extended definition of multiple elements. My claim is that myth is (1) a form of intentionality, which (2) provides an orientation for existence; (3) that this orientation is comprehensive of the life-world; (4) that it expresses itself in language; (5) that this language is highly condensed; (6) that it takes the form of a story; (7) that its language is neither literal nor metaphorical; (8) that myth is a special kind of apriori condition of theoretical thinking; (9) that myth's proper home is in the background of human existence; and (10) that it is part of the body.

First, myth is a form of intentionality. That means that it is not a representation. Moreover, it is primarily a form of the operative intentionality of the body-subject immersed in the life-world. Myth is not, therefore, an explanation, whether scientific (primitive or otherwise), theological, or philosophical. The mythic intention courses through the veins of life in the life-world and, consequently, forms part of the context or background for such theoretical operations as devising explanations.

Second, the mythic intention functions to provide an orientation for human existence. Imagine that Professor Smith arrives at Room 222 of the Humanities Building prepared to teach a seminar of senior undergraduates majoring in philosophy. She steps across the threshold into the room. As she does so, her gaze sweeps the room and takes in the fact that several small tables have been arranged in a long rectangular shape, one end of which is in front of the blackboard. She moves to the chair at that end of the rectangle and places her briefcase on the table. Her intention to teach meets the physical resources of the room and polarizes space in such a way as to achieve her aim in the most effective way possible. She does not, of course, think through her choice of location in any explicit way (she may do so, but that is not required); rather, the body-subject "lays down," as Merleau-Ponty would say, an oriented space in which the "choice" is obvious. The chair is given to her as "that on which to sit," the table as a "that on which to place my notes and my elbows," and the location at one end of the tables as a "place from which to see and be seen easily and to have ready access to the blackboard." On the other hand, when she returns to the classroom some hours later to retrieve her coat, which she left on the side of the tables opposite the door, her retrieval intention polarizes space in a different way. Chairs and tables become "obstacles to be circumambulated" in order to reach the coat. Like the teaching intention or the retrieving intention, the mythic intention provides an orientation for action.

Third, the mythic intention is distinguished from perceptual, affective, motor, and linguistic intentionalities in that it relies on an integration of the clues they offer to achieve a comprehensive orientation in the life-world. Myth intends the life-world as a whole. The teaching intention or the retrieval intention mentioned above are narrow, specific intentions which already presuppose and take place within an oriented world.

Linguistics has shown that individual words do not have meanings. The meaning of a word is given once the word is used in the wider context of a sentence. Some have argued that a sentence, not a word, is the smallest possible unit of meaning. This claim is analogous to the claim of Gestalt psychologists that the smallest element of perception is not a sense datum but a figure against a background. The meaning of a sentence, in turn, can be further specified in the context of a paragraph, the paragraph in the chapter, the chapter in a book, and a book in a literary tradition. The meaning of a part is understood against the background of a whole. Indeed, without a whole a part cannot be a part.

Analogously, our experiences of ourselves, of others, and of the natural order make increasing, if never perfect, sense as they are located in ever more inclusive contexts until the context of all contexts, a world, is reached. Thus, Stephen Daedalus, in Joyce's *Portrait of the Artist as a Young Man*, tries to make sense of his life by listing a sequence of ever more comprehensive contexts in

which his life is lived: Class of elements, Clongowes Wood College, Sallins, Country Kildare, Ireland, Europe, The World, The
Universe.

This spatial comprehensiveness is complemented by a temporal
one. Suppose I decide to plant tomatoes. This decision precipitates
a series of actions: driving to the nursery to buy seeds, going to my
garage to get a spade, digging in the soil to loosen it, folding fertil-
izer into the soil, making a shallow trough in the soil, placing seeds
in the trough, covering the seeds with soil, watering the soil.
Doubtless, what I do during two to three hours in my back yard
can be broken down into an indefinitely large number of relatively
distinct acts. Yet if someone accosted me while I was connecting
the garden hose to the hydrant and inquired what I was doing, I
would reply, "Planting tomatoes," despite the fact that I am twenty
yards away from the garden box and have neither tomatoes nor
tomato seeds in my hand. The tomato-planting intention arcs
across that list of distinct activities and binds them together into a
temporal whole or, perhaps more accurately, the distinct acts are
differentiated out of and generated by the tomato-planting intention. So soon as I intend to plant tomatoes, the required actions are
summoned in an effective sequence, provided I have some basic
skill as a gardener. Moreover, my answer "planting tomatoes"
retrotends my act of buying seeds an hour earlier and protends my
future acts of weeding, continued watering, and spraying with
insecticide to which my undertaking commits me. What "planting
tomatoes" does in binding together a limited range of activities, the
mythic intention does for the whole of the life-world, telling me
where I am, where I came from, and where I am going.

Myth does not, however, simply make possible periodic acts
of private self-gathering, as existentialists thinkers are inclined to
believe; the life-world embraces what reflection distinguishes as
self, society, and nature. Hence, in relation to the social aspect,
mythic intention may indicate whether my journey is fundamentally alone or inextricably bound up with others. It may identify
membership in social units and lay down social institutions, customs, and geographical boundaries. It may inform me whether my
relationship to others will be one of competition or cooperation; it
can polarize a moral terrain. Myth also "defines" nature, telling
me and others whether nature is to be regarded, as in some preliterate societies, as a brother, sister, mother, father, or as a machine;
whether it is to be worshiped or studied; whether it is to be nur-

tured or exploited; whether it can be known or not; whether it is perfect as it is or improvable with the help of human technologies; and whether it is real or unreal, temporal or fixed. This telling, indicating, identifying, and defining, however, are largely tacit. Since myth is primarily about the whole of the life-world, I prefer to use a different term, "mythlette," for tales with a narrower scope, for example, the story of how the deer got its white tail.

Fourth, the mythic intention expresses itself in language. We already saw that speaking, along with perception, feeling, and movement, is a basic intentionality or mode of existence of the body-subject. Spoken or written myth is the linguistic expression of the mythic intention of the body-subject trying to secure its grip upon the world it intends. Words provide some degree of distance from and highlight the most significant features of the life-world, giving it an increased coherence and stability. Words communicate with others and, thus, consolidate the life-world as a shared, social world. The linguistic grip enhances existence in the life-world, makes that life more effective. That a mythic intention can be lived prior to its articulation explains the appearance of the Timaeus late in Plato's career. The implications of his tacit participation in a certain life-world came to speech and reflection only gradually as he sought for his theory of forms the wider coherence and persuasiveness which only myth could provide.

Fifth, the language of myth is highly condensed. This is made necessary because the mythic intention aims at a comprehensive grasp of the system self-others-nature. A life-world full of meaning, both linguistic and prelinguistic, is, therefore, packed into a brief tale. This semantic density accounts also for the ambiguity of mythic language. It constitutes a virtually inexhaustible source for subsequent thematizations. The various anthropological, literary, philosophical, pyschoanalytic, sociological, and theological interpretations of a myth are so many attempts to unpack the black hole of meaning. These theoretical treatments of myth abstract from its concrete meaning, remove some of its ambiguity, and make it more determinate.

Sixth, the literary form of myth as language is a story. While traditional characterizations of myth have almost always made reference to its story form, we encountered in Chapter 3 several thinkers who identified myth with nonnarrative forms. Moreover, even when myth is said to be a story, the functionalist approach taken by scholars in recent years tends to endow form with no special significance and to assimilate narrative form to nonnarrative functions. Viewing myth as an explanation is one such example.

William Poteat has noted that human speech ranges from the groans of pain and the moans of sexual passion, on the one hand, to the most sophisticated theoretical propositions, on the other.[15] Between these extremes, I would argue, lie a variety of linguistic forms, each having its own logic and its own degree of personal backing. Perhaps each is the linguistic expression of a particular mode of existence. Along this range the story is a form intermediate between a groan and a theory. It remains closer to vitality, to feeling, to the body, to concrete engagement in the life-world than does theory, in which distance from the life-world is increased and according to whose conventions explicit reference to the life-world is prohibited.

A story reflects in its very form the temporality which is the substance of human existence. According to David Carr, however, this claim is precisely what has been denied by a number of literary theorists, among them Louis Mink, Hayden White, Roland Barthes, and Frank Kermode.[16] Although they differ in the details of their positions, they seem to stress the discontinuity between life and art, affirming that narrative structure is an artificial literary order produced by the creative imagination and imposed upon a chaotic life to which it is extrinsic. Even Paul Ricoeur, who, Carr notes, says life is in "disarray" rather than chaotic and possesses a "pre-narrative structure," eventually concludes that narrative is a kind of metaphoric redescription "as if" life were a story. Ricoeur says, "The ideas of beginning, middle, and end are not taken from experience: They are not traits of real action but effects of poetic ordering."[17] According to Hayden White, life is more properly characterized "in the way that annals and chronicles suggest, either as a mere sequence without beginning or end or as sequences of beginnings that only terminate and never conclude."[18]

Carr, by contrast, with help from Husserl, Heidegger, Merleau-Ponty, Barbara Hardy, Peter Munz, Wilhelm Schapp, Alasdair MacIntyre, and Frederick Olafson, looks for narrative structure in ordinary life experiences rather than in the aesthetic-cognitive activities of creating novels or writing histories. He examines, first of all, Husserl's account of the relatively passive act of listening to a melody and then the active case of serving the ball in tennis. Both instances involve an ongoing retention of the immediate past and a protention of the future. Retention and protention are, for Husserl,

a matter of the primary memory and anticipation rather than recollection and expectation, which are secondary. While the latter
are more conscious and reflective, the former are prereflective. In
other words, as Carr notes, the horizon-focus structure Gestalt
psychology found to be fundamental in spatial perception occurs
also in the experience of time. The shifting retention and protention achieve a "temporal grasp" of the whole act or event (one
which can, of course, be disappointed and is constantly revised),
whose completion brings about a "closure," which, along with the
undertaking of the event or act, provides a beginning, middle, and
end to the event or act and distinguishes it externally from all others. Carr concludes: "The bedrock of human events, then, is not
sequence but configured sequence."[19] As he notes, pure sequence in
life is an abstraction created by reflection and read back into experience in the same way sense data were created out of the figure-
background structure of perception and read back into the origins
of perception.

Beyond that, Carr argues that ordinary experience is "inter-
nally articulated" in a variety of patterns (suspension-resolution,
means-ends, departure-arrival, departure-return, repetition, and
problem-solution) and that, like narrative, we experience ourselves as characters or agents, narrators, and audience. If, to use
my own previous example, someone asks me what I am doing, I
might well reply by telling the story of planting tomatoes, which I
am acting out. Sometimes, as Carr notes, we tell (narrator) stories
to ourselves (audience), perhaps silently, in acts of "self-explica-
tion" or "self-clarification."[20] We do so not simply subsequent to
an action but in the midst of the action.

In such longer stories as "writing a book, getting an education, or raising a child" interruptions occur. Carr says that this
necessitates reflection to help reorient ourselves following a break
and expectation in the form of deliberate planning, instead of
mere anticipation. In other words, life is structured as a series of
overlapping projects, sometimes requiring an active intentionality,
but held together ultimately by the operative intentionality of the
body-subject.

The conclusion Carr reaches is that "narrative has its first role
in the pre-literary structuring and shaping of real life, before it is
employed in literary embodiments . . . " and that literary narratives "exist within and arise out of a real world already organized
in narrative fashion." Indeed, he claims that literary narratives

get their narrative structure from the human world in which
they have their origin. It is to this origin that they owe not only
their capacity to represent the real world . . . but also the very
idea of undertaking such a representation.[21]

Carr believes, correctly in my estimation, that those whose
views he is criticizing view the reality on which narrative structure
is imposed as a purely physical reality resembling the universe as
imagined by positivist science rather than the human world—or,
as I would prefer to say, the life-world of self-others-nature—
already imbued with values and meanings, in which we find ourselves. This insight penetrates to the hidden commitment of such
persons to the inner-outer split which lies at the foundation of
modernity. Moreover, the reflexive tendency to fracture the lived
world by abstraction into a chaotic, material substance given
order by externally imposed mental forms bears the marks of the
omnipresent myth of the Timaeus.

Seventh, myth is not metaphorical. This claim flies in the face
of virtually all modern interpreters of myth. For those interpreters
the rescue of myth seemed to demand a metaphorical reading. If
myth is not literally about gods and goddesses but about society,
nature, ideas, possibilities for human existence, or the unconscious, then, necessarily, myth must be metaphorical. In recent
decades a consensus has been reached among many philosophers
around a new and more positive understanding of metaphor. This
understanding has been applied to both scientific and religious
language, including myth. Thus, the view that myths are
metaphorical has been strengthened.

Max Black's famous essay "Models and Metaphors," which
helped to form that consensus, distinguishes the new view of
metaphor from two traditional ones. Black, first of all, rejects
both the "substitution" theory, according to which a metaphor
takes the place of some literal expression in order either to fill a
vocabulary gap or to provide a decorative element which brings
aesthetic pleasure. Next, he rejects the "comparison" theory,
which regards metaphor as an elliptical simile. For example, in the
metaphorical statement "a geometrical proof is like a mousetrap"
the comparison theory holds that both the "tenor" ("a geometrical proof") and the "vehicle" ("mousetrap") have certain specifiable and objectively given features in common. Both the substitution and the comparison theories imply that literal expressions are

temporally and logically prior to metaphorical ones and that the latter can be translated into the former without loss of meaning. This amounts to an attempt to reduce background to foreground. In the final analysis, meaningful language is, in this view, literal language. To be meaningful, then, the language of myth would have to be either literal language or translatable into literal language, an impossibility on modern premises.

Black's own theory, however, is consonant with the current consensus, which he helped to create, that metaphor is not a substitute for a literal term but has its own unique functions. It does not express an antecedently spelled out similarity between two things but gives a first articulation in language of an original insight. Two terms (vehicle and tenor) juxtaposed in a metaphorical statement, along with their specifiable and unspecifiable connotations, "interact" so as to create a novel meaning, which is greater than the sum of their separate meanings. Analogies, rather than providing the foundation for metaphors, are derived by further differentiation and refinement of metaphors.

The new consensus, while assigning special functions to metaphor, continues to assume the literal-metaphorical distinction. That distinction itself, however, has become problematic. Walter Ong, for example, suggests that the word literal is itself a metaphor; the concept occurs only in those cultures having an alphabet—that is, in which letters represent, are metaphors for, the sounds of speech. William Poteat elaborates on this insight:

> We have seen that there can be only a metaphorical hence no literal meaning of the word "literal," since, to be etymologically strict, a literal meaning would be "taken by the letters." But l.i.t.e.r.a.l. are not a word. If then I were to wish to say, "He was literally at the end of his rope," and mean and you took me to mean, "He was hanging by a strand of twisted hemp," this would occur only because you and I have tacitly agreed to take "literally" metaphorically, that is, to take the mere letters, l.i.t.e.r.a.l., as a word.[22]

Some postmodernists go so far as to claim that all language is metaphorical. Terry Eagleton, in characterizing the Yale School of Deconstruction generally and Paul de Man in particular, says, "All language, as de Man rightly perceives, is ineradicably metaphorical. . . . "[23]

There is, however, a logical problem here. "Metaphorical"

and "literal" are, as one might expect Deconstructionists to appreciate, binary opposites. Each is defined largely by the ways in which it differs from the other. If all meanings of "literal" are said to be "metaphorical," then what can "metaphorical" mean? We can, of course, resort to such meanings of "literal" as "the first meaning of a word" or "the most common or obvious meaning of a word" and such meanings of "metaphorical" as "the fresh, novel, or shocking use of a word," but these historical or psychological definitions are not devoid of practical difficulties and are epistemologically insignificant. Owen Barfield once suggested that "figural" be used of language prior to the differentiation out of it of "metaphorical" and "literal." This move, rather than solving the problem in the terms in which it is posed, points to the largely tacit operation of language and its ultimate unspecifiability.

The second problem with the identification of the language of myth as metaphorical appears from the perspective of the philosophical analysis of our actual use of language. William Poteat examines the saying of "Give us this day our daily bread" by committed worshipers reciting the Lord's Prayer in the context of a Christian liturgy in a church sanctuary. He imagines that these worshipers are observed by persons for whom acquiring bread means either baking one's own bread or going to the bakery shop and placing some money on the counter in the expectation of being handed a loaf of bread. Assuming the role of such persons, Poteat asks:

> But what are we to make of these people on their knees, saying aloud, it appears, to no one in particular, and certainly to no bakery shop clerk: "Give us this day our daily bread." If we are complacent, we will say that these people are confused or benighted. They *think* they are (literally?) asking for bread when they could not be. If we are *not* complacent, we might suppose that their language bears in some figurative way upon *the literal* state of affairs described in terms of the above two cases—in suggesting which we are not forgetting that "give me my daily bread" spoken to the bakery clerk is direct, serious, and more likely to be efficacious than the "figurative" language of those on their knees. The literal/figurative distinction still has authority over us. What is literal and direct is what is serious and real; all the rest of our talk is, however pleasing and even irresistible, secondary or tertiary. Nevertheless, if we are particularly acute, we may come to see that distinguishing between

shopping for bread and "praying for bread" by invoking the literal/figurative distinction sheds no light. It only reinforces our modernist prejudice. The weight and force of the words "Give me this day our daily bread," uttered in the setting of prayer, are exactly what they are and not some other thing: As direct and unequivocal as can be, which no translation can improve or further legitimize. These words are among those that give form to the world in which I live.[24]

Likewise, a person prereflectively using in the appropriate context the language of a myth he or she is living out draws no distinction between the metaphorical or literal meanings or uses of the words spoken. The mythic intention which issues in speech intends *the very world* embodied in the words spoken. The distinction is made in reflection as a second-order or third-order operation and in the service of a theoretical interest. In the context of modernity, that theoretical interest will involve segregating the words which apply to one's inner experience from those which bear on the so-called "real" world. To maintain that myth is metaphorical is to persist, even if unwittingly, in supporting the modern, dualistic agenda.

Eighth, myth is an apriori condition of theoretical thinking. A moment's reflection will make this obvious. In order to theorize, a person, so far as we know, must be alive. More than that, he or she must have an oriented world in which to become literate and practice speaking, writing, reading, and thinking under the tutelage of skilled persons functioning in institutions in an organized society. Such an oriented world requires myth as the primordial orientation upon which secondary orientations and organizings rely and without which the secondary operations would not be able to get underway.

In Chapter 4 we were acquainted with Polanyi's epistemology, according to which all feats of knowing involve a reliance upon specifiable and unspecifiable clues which enable us to attend to some integrated whole which is their joint meaning. The clues are mostly tacit; the whole which they mean is largely explicit. In a subsequent moment, however, the whole can be shifted to the tacit dimension where it guides an analysis of that whole which takes place largely explicitly. In perception, for example, we may integrate such clues as circles, dots, lines, and ellipses, arranged in a particular way, to recognize the physiognomy of a rabbit drawn on a page. Tacit reliance on the rabbit (the whole), in turn, directs an analysis of the figure into ears, feet, tail, eye, and trunk (the parts).

The world, as we have seen, is the horizon of all horizons. It is the ultimate context for all human activities, including thinking. Myth, as we have seen, is the primordial and comprehensive grasp of this life-world and, therefore, is always present in the tacit dimension to orient and guide all reflective analysis. Like a Kantian apriori, myth is presumptively universal. Also, it is necessary for making judgments, although this necessity is not merely a logical one. It is a biological-psychological-logical one—that is, it is a lived necessity preceding the distinction in theory between the logical and the psychological-biological. That means that myth cuts across the analytic-synthetic distinction, too. On the other hand, myth is not a "Category of the Understanding," a transcendental condition for some possible experience. It is an existential condition arising in actual experience. This is but another way of saying that the subject of experience, of judgment, and of myth is not a transcendental ego but a concrete, living, bodily human being. I prefer, therefore, to say that myth is a Wordsworthian apriori. Wordsworth wrote that "the child is father of the man."[25] The facts, values, symbols, images, stories, myths, ideologies, styles, skills, etc., that are absorbed during the uncritical years of childhood constitute the deepest layers of a tacit apriori we bring to any human act in the present, including theoretical analysis and speculation. Indeed, we do not merely *bring* this tacit apriori to the present; we *are* all this we bring. In Polanyian terms we "indwell" or "embody" it. For Merleau-Ponty, it is carried forward in the "habits" of the body-subject.

Ninth, I wish here merely to reiterate the claim made at the end of Chapter 4—namely, that myth belongs primarily to the background of human existence. It functions prereflectively as an orientation to that most comprehensive context which guides and gives meaning to the panoply of activities taking place in that context or world. The claim concerning its largely tacit character has special relevance to modernity in which the functioning of myth is not and cannot be recognized, but is applicable as well to preliterate societies for whom the explicit recollection of myth took place under controlled conditions on special ritual occasions.

Tenth, myth is part of the body. Clearly, this makes no sense if the body is a Cartesian machine or any of its more contemporary, electronic cousins. It does make sense, however, if, as Merleau-

Ponty observes, the body is not an object among objects but is a subject and if, as I have claimed, myth is a form of operative intentionality of that body-subject. The relation of myth to the body can be understood with the help of several distinctions, drawn by Merleau-Ponty, between the body and objects. In each case myth shares the same characteristics as the body.[26]

1. The body, unlike an object, does not leave me. I can walk away from tables and trees but cannot walk away from my body. Tools can be picked up and used for specific and temporary tasks, but when a task is completed, the tool is put aside. Objects can even disappear completely from sight, touch, or utilization. The body, on the other hand, never loses or changes its relationship to me. It is never discarded. It is always with me. It is me.

The same is true of myth. We may temporarily give consideration to a point of view espoused by a partner in dialogue or debate and, in reading a book, we may entertain a theory being advanced by its author. These views are usually put aside, however, when reading and conversation terminate. Even on those occasions when we embrace a theory, creed, or ideology (products of theoretical reflection) as our own, our commitment to it is apt to endure for only a matter of months, years, or decades. Myth, on the other hand, like a native language, is absorbed early, preconsciously, and/or prereflectively. It becomes a permanent acquisition. Myth is never merely entertained, never used temporarily and for a limited purpose. It is part of our identity. Sometimes thinkers speak of language as a tool. Strictly speaking, neither myth nor language is a tool; both are part of the body.

2. Merleau-Ponty points out that the body, unlike an object, "defies exploration." An object can be placed in front of me, arrayed before me, situated totally within my field of vision. I can take it apart, open it up, explore it fully. My body, however, is only partially accessible to my sight or touch. It resists investigation. The movement of the muscles of my eyes *as I look* at a flower, for example, are forever hidden to me. Even in a mirror I cannot catch my living glance. Moreover, the body is not given to me from some perspective, as is a sculpture or a building; it *is* that perspective— and a permanent one—from which things appear to me.

Similarly, myth lies in the corpuscular and crepuscular dimensions of our knowing and doing. The theorists discussed in Chapter 4 probably are not aware of their reliance upon the Timaeus and Genesis. Even when we are made aware of that reliance and essay critically to examine the myth we may be living, we catch only a fleeting glimpse of it. The life-world of meaning-being which the myth so densely expresses recedes into the inarticulate, the bodily. Our theories and explanations of myth never exhaust it. My own theory of myth is no exception. It has at least this one virtue— namely, building into the definition the fact that myth, like the body, defies exploration.

3. Unlike objects, the body is affective. It feels. "My foot hurts," says Merleau-Ponty, does not mean that the foot is the last (before reaching me) in a chain of external, objective causes, analogous to the tip of a nail or tack as it penetrates the skin. The foot itself is the seat of the pain. It does not cause the pain; it undergoes the pain.

Myth, too, is affective and, therefore, part of the body. The Western philosophical tradition has wanted to separate intellect and feeling. For Plato, true knowledge comes when we, among other things, rise above passion. For Descartes, genuine knowledge is achieved when the intellect operates alone, without feeling, imagination, or perception. Theories, consequently, are thought to inhabit the rarified air of a realm transcending ordinary life. Such a picture is, of course, a false one, as recent studies in the history and philosophy of science attest. If Archimedes' joyful "Eureka" is not sufficient evidence, then consider the feelings of aesthetic appreciation prompted in mathematicians and physicists by the elegance or beauty of a formula or equation or the intellectual passion which fuels the attempt to overthrow an established theory for one initially regarded as preposterous.

Myths, unlike theories, have always been regarded as involving feeling. Surely that is one of the reasons why Enlightenment thinkers sought to rid the world of myths. Far from occupying the lofty reaches of the theoretical intellect, myth is intimately involved in the tragic-comic exigencies of embodied existence, pervaded by insistent and undeniable feelings and passions.

Earlier on, I said that myth as a special form of intentionality is distinct from motor, perceptual, and affective intentionalities. In fact, these intentionalities, distinguished only in reflection, are integrated in a primordial, corporeal synergy. Mythic intentions, consequently, are accompanied by affective ones. Mythic affect is obvious in the heightened sense of being alive experienced, for example, by Native American peoples on those periodic occasions when they gather in a hogan, clearing, or longhouse for a pow-wow or more traditional ceremonial in which traditional myths are reenacted. The affective dimensions of myth help explain why it has been so frequently connected to ritual.

4. According to some psychologists, bodies differ from objects by dint of having "kinesthetic sensations," a phrase Merleau-Ponty regards as a misleading description of what he prefers to call "the power of original movement." By this he means that it is unnecessary to locate one's body in space, grasp it, and move it to another point in space, as one does an object. As soon as the intention to move the flower vase to the center of the mantelpiece arises, the arm is already on its way toward the vase, before thought finds the arm, gives it orders, and guides it in the completion of the task. This is but one of the many ways in which the body-subject is ahead of thought, taking root in concrete situations.

Again, the same is true of myth. Whether one is critiquing or developing a philosophical theory, launching a murder investigation, writing a novel, or undertaking a scientific inquiry, there is no need to "locate" myth and instruct it in how to orient us for these enterprises. As part of the body, myth is already there ahead of reflection. It is part of what makes any such instructions possible and what makes them superfluous.

5. Pscychologists, says Merleau-Ponty, speak, again misleadingly, of the body as capable of "double sensations"—for example, if with my left hand I touch my right hand, the right hand (the object) is itself feeling (like a subject). When an object, on the other hand, say a fork, "touches" my body, the fork neither feels nor catches my body in an act of feeling.

The phenomenon of double sensations does, I believe, exhibit parallels with myth, even if they are not exact. Suppose that in order to analyze a myth which I have embodied, I indwell a theory (say pscyhoanalysis) by means of which to conduct the analysis of that myth. Theory and myth are analogous to the left and right hands, respectively, in the example in the previous paragraph. Not only does the theory "feel" (interpret, analyze, take into account) the myth but the myth "feels" (affects and effects the "construction," choice, and application of) the theory. The myth, as part of my body, both "feels" or prehends the theory and is prehended by it.

My claim that myth is part of the body makes sense also on Polanyian premisses. Although Polanyi devotes little or no attention to an anthropology of the body, the epistemological functions of his theory of the tacit dimension are similar to those of Merleau-Ponty's body-subject. Just as, for Polanyi, all acts of explicit knowing have a tacit coefficient, so, for Merleau-Ponty, both reflection and perception are rooted in our bodily being-in-the-world. Polanyi's "from-to" structure of tacit knowing has the vectorial thrust of intentionality. Moreover, operative intentionality is hidden from view, as is much of what occurs in the tacit dimension. Finally, the tacit dimension is inseparable, in Polanyi's thought, from "indwelling" and "embodiment."

One of the implications of Polanyi's thinking is that the body's parameters are not rigid and fixed but are flexible and expandable like an accordion or, to use an organic analogy, a lung. Taking in air is a condition for the lung's expansion. In Chapter 4 we saw how, for Polanyi, the body expands itself through the taking in of tools—for example, a hammer. We attend subsidiarily to the impact of the hammer's handle upon the hand in order to attend focally to the impact of the hammer's head upon the nail. The incorporation of the hammer into the body is accomplished by "pouring ourselves into the subsidiary awareness of particulars"[27] generated by the hand-handle contact. On this view, the body becomes whatever is relied upon in the performance of an act. Body is the from of the from-to structure of knowing-doing.

The indwelling of clues involved in the use of a hammer may be temporary. It is like a night in a motel or a week in a beachfront cottage. For the carpenter, by contrast, the hammer is used daily; it is home. Moreover, the skills involved in their use become a relatively permanent acquisition. Thus, the concert pianist takes out insurance on his or her hands; that is where the skill of playing the piano is located. Perhaps "embodiment" is preferable to "indwelling" in the latter cases, although no sharp line divides the two.

Analogously, our reliance on theories, creeds, ideologies is a relatively more temporary indwelling, while our reliance upon myth is a more permanent embodiment. Again, myth is part of the body.

Having now laid out my own theory, I wish to sharpen it a bit further in relation to that of Sanford Krolick, author of *Recollective Resolve: A Phenomenological Understanding of Time and Myth*.[28] We set out from roughly the same place but, owing in part to different aims, soon diverge. Krolick adopts, as do I, an existential phenomenological method and understands myth as rooted in the life-world. He also adopts Merleau-Ponty's anonymous, prepersonal body-subject, emphasizing its distinctively human tendency to express and embody itself in language.

This philosophical anthropology, however, is grafted to a Heideggerian analysis of human existence as *Dasein*. As a being-in the-world which is also a project-in-the-making, *Dasein* is fundamentally temporal in nature. *Dasein*, however, becomes lost in the objectifications of thought; forgetful of its "thrownness," its "facticity," its finite existential grounding, it falls into inauthenticity by permitting itself to be determined by nobody in particular (what Heidegger calls "the One" and Krolick describes as "the nameless and faceless character of the public domain"[29]); and fails to achieve the wholeness of its full potential. *Dasein* must recover its authentic self by a temporal "self-gathering" in which past, present, and future are "recollected" in a fresh resolve to face the future in an anxiety-filled quest for full self-realization.

Krolick's original contribution comes when he asserts that while Heideggerian *Dasein* constitutes one form of authentic human existence, mythic existence constitutes another. Because mythic existence has been "eclipsed by our various literate and technical thematizations of experience,"[30] it is necessary to look to preliterate or newly literate cultures, in which oral-aural sensibilities dominate, where *Dasein* as mythmaker appears in "pristine form." He turns, therefore, to studies by anthropologists and historians of religions but insists that these studies "serve only an illustrative function"[31] in relation to his existential analysis.

Agreeing with Van der Leeuw that the essence of religion has to do with power, Krolick asserts that concern with power arises because the intentionality of "the primitive myth maker," itself a preconscious power, is "overwhelmed" by the "environment."[32] Because there is an intimate connection between power and the sacred, mythic existence necessarily has a religious dimension. Preliterate peoples cope with this environment by identifying with and projecting themselves into it in a variety of ways, including ritual reenactment. Myth makes use of "compact" and "plurivocal" language to "disclose the integrity and multidimensionality of mythic Dasein's orientation within the world."[33]

Identification with nature, says Krolick, entails identification with nature's "biocosmic rhythms," which leads "not to an intuition of time that is rectilinear, irreversible, and abstract, but rather to one that is concrete, periodic, and thus capable of repetition."[34] Stylistically, this "periodicity" expresses itself in mythic language as "repeated refrains, choruses, or phrases in the story."[35] In mythic existence, then, time is primarily an oscillation between the present and a past which is to be repeated, and even future possibilities are "*empowered* by a fundamentally constitutive past."[36] The future is not, therefore, "an ever-receding horizon of infinite progress" but "a finite set of meaningful possibilities made actual only on the ground of an enabling past (or tradition) that is periodically 'gathered up' (*aufgehoben*) within the present moment of decision (*Augenblick*)" in what amounts to a unique, mythic mode of existence called "repetition or recollective resolve."[37]

Obviously, there is much in Krolick's theory with which I am in agreement; however, I will focus here on the differences. First, Krolick's view appears to limit myth to preliterate or newly literate societies living in direct and extensive contact with nature and overwhelmed by it. This restriction arbitrarily rules out both the Timaeus and Genesis, which are commonly regarded as myths. Krolick's approach is like defining "religion" in terms of theism and, consequently, denying that Theravada Buddhism, Taoism, and the Hinduism of the Upanishads are religions.

The Timaeus is certainly concerned with nature but is hardly overwhelmed by it. Indeed, the stories of Daedalus and Prometheus, which probably circulated orally long before being put into writing, reflect a Greek life-world situated in cities, in which confidence in the human capacity to deal effectively with nature had grown strong and the daily realities are other people and social institutions. The "Ode to Man" chorus in Sophocles' "Antigone," which was written decades after Aeschylus' "Prometheus Bound" but before Plato's *Timaeus*, sings the praises of man, the "prodigy," who uses the net to catch fish, the bridle to tame the horse and bull, the sail to harness the wind, the plow to till the ground, the house to keep out bad weather, and the law to govern human conduct. Indeed, he "conquers with his arts" virtually everything "save Death alone"; even here "where cure was despaired of, he has found one."[38] Even if later events in the play qualify this man-as-nature's-conqueror ideology, man is hardly depicted as overwhelmed by nature.

Genesis, on the other hand, although it appreciates nature as God's handiwork, makes man the crown of creation. This is not surprising given the traditional Hebrew preoccupation with social and political concerns. Even before the P-account of creation was written, the psalmist, awestruck at the moon and stars, asks, "What is man that thou shouldst remember him" and answers, "Yet thou has made him little less that a god."[39] Krolick's view also seems to overlook the work of Malinowski among the Melanesians and that of subsequent social scientists, all of whom point to the social functions of myth.

Krolick's selectiveness is amply illustrated in his treatment of the *Enuma Elish*. He relates Henri Frankfort's description of the alluvial action of the Tigris and Euphrates to characters and events in the Mesopotamian myth.[40] On the other hand, Cornelius Loew's interpretation, contained in another of Frankfort's works (*Before Philosophy*), shows how the tale concerns the sociopolitical transition from organized cities and towns to city-states, then from city-states to a national empire. Clearly, mythic existence cannot be linked exclusively to preoccupation with the natural environment, overwhelming or otherwise. In the system self-others-nature, the social world is sometimes dominant.

Second, Krolick's claims about mythic time are confusing, partly because of his use of a variety of terms which are not adequately distinguished and which seem to operate as synonyms— for example, circularity, periodicity, aeonic, repetition, return, retrieval, pendularity, and oscillation. His purpose is to establish, by contrast to Heidegger, that self-gathering, the act which makes existence authentic, does not require leaving the past behind but can take place in periodic rituals in which one looks backward to mythic tales of origin to find exemplars and possibilities for living. In so doing, however, he appears to find an exclusive and necessary link among periodic ritual activity, periodicity in myths, and a circular view of time.

By "periodicity," for example, he means that "the myth maker's life-world is grasped according to the beginning and ending of various biosocial-cosmic cycles."[41] He recognizes, however, that the *Heilsgeschichte* of the Bible is not readily assimilable to his theory and, consequently, attempts to establish periodicity in the Bible by pointing to such phrases as "In the beginning God created the heavens and the earth" (Genesis 1:1) and "In the beginning was the word," as well as to the mythic dimensions of Jesus' ministry. I would argue that while the "events" of such a beginning may be appropriated repeatedly in periodic ritual reenactments, we are not to think of either the creation of the world or the ministry of Jesus as recurring on a regular or even an irregular basis.

"Beginning" does, indeed, mark off a temporal period, but in the case of at least much of the biblical tradition, such a period is not to be understood as "a recurring cycle" but as embracing the whole of an irreversible time. Thus, William H. Poteat distinguishes two conceptions of myth in the West. One has "its origin in primitive ritual, primitive cosmology" and is associated with Greece. The other, which he terms "eschatological myth," is Hebraic.[42] While the former lays down eternal patterns, the latter launches a unique history. Just as a person's birth occurred on one day only and yet may be celebrated annually, so in both cases the "originary events" may be repeatedly reappropriated and may be constitutive (in some sense and degree) for human existence. In the first kind, however, the return to mythic origins is likely to occur in public rituals and to require a strict imitation of acts performed by the gods or heroes—for example, the Navajo notion that women must sit with their legs under them because Changing Woman did so at the beginning.[43] Eschatological myth, in my view, is not so strictly tied to rituals and often functions to redirect persons in a forward direction, supplying them not so much with precise models to be imitated in endlessly repeated time but with fresh inspiration and courage to face a future that is novel, open, and unknown.

Third, the return to mythic origins by way of memory and reenactment is both conscious and reflective. In Husserl's terms, it is a matter of "recollection-expectation" rather than of the preconscious and prereflective "retention-protention." The latter, however, characterizes our most fundamental inherence in the dynamic system of self-others-nature. That life-world contains a rich and complex array of motor, perceptual, affective, linguistic, social, and natural resources for apprehending time as a variety of overlapping patterns and projects. These resources would include not only diurnal, lunar, and seasonal (solar) rhythms, agricultural patterns (seed time and harvest), and somatic periodicities (menstruation), but also events experienced as special and unique, such as the birth of one's child, that child's initiation or marriage, and one's own death. Moreover, there are as many, if not more, occasions for looking forward as looking backward, such as the urgency of getting the next meal on the table—a concern that would be all the stronger for the most technologically primitive peoples living in direct contact with nature—not to mention the preparations one may be making for the upcoming festival or military campaign or trip to collect salt.

In relation to this tangle of concrete times both the curvilinear and rectilinear *views* of time, insofar as they attempt to provide a *comprehensive* grasp of time, are equally abstract. Which elements of the life-world are thematized in reflection may simply reflect which elements are dominant in the system of self-others-nature. For preliterate peoples living close to nature or farmers attuned to the agricultural cycle, the repetitive features of the life-world will be abstracted and made constitutive of a view of time. For nomads on the move or societies constituted by social-religious-political events like the Exodus or Covenant at Sinai, the unique and irreversible will take precedence. Indeed, given the panoply of concrete, lived, interwoven temporalities there is no reason why there should be merely two kinds of existence (one looking back and one looking forward) or two views of time (one repeated and one irreversible). Such a limitation merely perpetuates the over-simplification of the life-world dictated to thought by the logic of excluded middle. In my view, temporalities and existences may come in a tropical profusion of varieties.

Given that the ethnographic material Krolick uses comes from the Tangu, Melanesians, Australian aborigines, Canaque, Caledonians, Apaches, ancient Egyptians, ancient Mesopotamians, Tiv, Karuru, Nuer, and Lugbara, and given that his theory ignores the Timaeus and cannot encompass Genesis, I suspect that this material is constitutive of that theory and not, as he insists, merely illustrative.

His use of Van der Leeuw to speak about the essence of religion is also telling. The reader will recall that Van der Leeuw is mentioned in Chapter 4 as an exponent of that approach to the study of religion (the old phenomenology of religion) which assumes that religion has a universal and definable essence underlying the particulars of its various cultural manifestations. That view seems to have influenced Krolick's search for a universal essence of mythic existence. For my part, I share with historians of religion a skepticism about the existence of such universal religious essences. Put positively, I believe that mythic existences can differ meaningfully, not merely incidentally, as do the life-worlds they articulate.

Finally, Krolick's preference for Heidegger over Merleau-Ponty results in too great an emphasis, especially with respect to preliterate societies, on the "existential function" of myth—that is, moments in which past, present, and future are integrated in acts of self-gathering. Others and nature become significant only insofar as they enter the concerns of the self as *Dasein*. The reader will recall that following Heidegger led Bultmann to an "inside-middle" emphasis (see Chapter 2). If for a mythmaker nature itself cannot be an object of interest, it is not surprising that for Krolick myth would have little or nothing to do with science.

Applied to the battle between the forces of Marduk and the forces of Tiamat, the heart of Mesopotamian myth, Krolick's approach leads him to interpret the story as reflecting the structure of an act of self-gathering. Thus, Ea becomes the past, Kingu (the defeated general) the present, and Marduk (the victorious general) the future. "The ancient Mesopotamian," says Krolick, "experienced this myth as a means of returning to the primordial ground . . . of his existence."[44] "Experienced" seems to do for the Mesopotamians what Bultmann did for persons in the New Testament—namely, turn them into twentieth-century philosophers.

I have no wish to deny the significance of the shift from preliteracy to literacy. By indwelling and relying upon the articulate forms made possible by writing (such as theories), we have certainly modified, for both good and ill, our ways of reflecting in particular and our ways of being-in-the-world more generally. Perhaps that is why, in putting forward my own views, I have spoken not of "mythic existence" but of "mythic intention" and "myth dependence." Krolick's aim, however, as he makes clear in his "Introduction," is to do a phenomenology of religion, whereas I wish to point to the ways in which science and philosophy also are indebted to myth. Thus, rather than framing a theory of myth in terms that are opposed to Heidegger's views, I would expect to find both continuity and discontinuity between Heidegger and, for example, the Melanesians—that is, I would expect to discover ways in which Heidegger, too, is dependent upon myth.

If retrieval of a mythic past is what is crucial to Krolick, then the difference between his mythic existence and my myth-dependency may actually be slight. Consider the case of the first *Critique* of Immanuel Kant. Kant wished to heal the division between the Rationalists (Descartes, Leibniz, and Spinoza) and the Empiricists (Locke, Berkeley, and Hume). His strategy was to say that both experience (sense perception) and knowledge (thought) contain a conceptual element (a nod to rationalism) and a sensuous element (a nod to empiricism). Knowledge, for example, results when the conceptual element and the more chaotic perceptual element (itself the result of a prior synthesis) are synthesized by the Transcendental Ego with the help of the Categories of the Understanding. Kant appears to be the very paradigm of a modern thinker. Indeed, he is sometimes called the "father of modern philosophy." Awash in abstract theoretical concepts, he has "seen through" (in principle) not only the simplistic mythical worlds of the preliterate past but even the empirical world of the scientists.

Appearances, however, are still sometimes deceiving. One has but to substitute "copy form" for "conceptual," "material" for "sensuous," "pure forms" for "categories," "craftsman" for "transcendental ego," "molded" or "shaped" for "synthesized," "intelligible world" for "transcendental," and "cosmos" for "knowledge" to recognize beneath the modern, subjectivist idiom the lineaments of the Timaeus. Is this not an unmistakable and potent retrieval of what is commonly viewed as the past (but which I would regard as an ongoing past and, therefore, an active present)? Perhaps a noteworthy difference between the modern philosopher and the preliterate mythmaker is that Kant cannot acknowledge and is probably not even aware of his dependency upon myth. That dependency is clearly there, however, as part of the myriad and ultimately unspecifiable tacit acceptances upon which relatively explicit thought is structurally reliant.

Ironically, the inability of modernists to acknowledge the dependency of theoretical thinking on myth is due, in part, to the extraordinary success of the Timaeus itself. The impersonal, uninteresting, self-effacing Craftsman and the relatively routine and mechanical manipulation of external constituents to construct an impersonal, composite, and essentially timeless world comprise a set of peculiarities which serve to discredit the story form of myth itself. In that regard, the Timaeus, itself a story, is the myth of the ending of myth—that is, the myth whose effect is to render myth invisible.

It will now be obvious to the reader that, whereas in Chapter 4 I merely described in a relatively noncommittal fashion the alternative theories emanating from Genesis and the Timaeus, in this chapter I have tipped my hand in favor of Genesis. The choice of existential phenomenology as the best framework for understanding myth is a conspicuous case in point. Its interest in temporality and in human existence set in a social and natural world that is real, its view of human knowledge as finite, and its confidence in experience (including sense perception freed from the Greek-based presupposition of sense data)[45] indicate its indebtedness to Hebraic culture and Genesis. Structuralism, on the other hand, with its fixed, explicit, universal structures organizing and explaining discrete, arbitrary, and chaotic elements is a recent descendent of the Timaeus. Phenomenology versus Structuralism, then, is the most recent guise under which the struggle of Genesis versus the Timaeus, discussed in Chapter 4, has taken place. Postmodernism, at least Derrida's brand of it, is simultaneously committed to the Timaeus in terms of its parasitic dependence upon ontological and epistemological dualism and to Genesis in terms of its critique of that commitment. Because the Timaeus is given priority, however, postmodernism tends to skepticism and relativism.

That I would acknowledge the particular mythic basis for my own theory of myth could have been expected in light of my criticism in Chapters 2 and 3 of the failure of modern myth theorists to do so. Indeed, I find myself in agreement with the Buddhist philosopher Kukai (eighth–ninth centuries), who neither replaced myth by philosophy nor equated myth with philosophy but sought to create a philosophy supportive of myth.[46] In my view, there is no other choice.

Are claims of knowledge, then, reduced to a blind, irrational faith in or an arbitrary choice between one myth rather than another? I do not think so. That question does, however, call for a consideration of the relation of myth to truth.


## MYTH AND TRUTH

The question of truth is a crucial one for locating a postcritical perspective in relation to a modern or ultramodern one. It is also crucial for anyone wishing to offer a more positive assessment of myth. If I have focused on the logical, ontological, and epistemological implications of myth and ignored its sociological, psychological, and religious functions, it is not because I wish to deny the latter. Myth is a many-splendored thing. The power of myth to succeed in its other functions, however, depends upon its being believed to be true in some sense. Modernity's position on this matter is clear: however useful myth may be in psychological or sociological terms, it is, in the final analysis, false or meaningless. More recently, some instrumentalists have said that it is neither true nor false. Modernity can hardly say otherwise. But what of a postcritical perspective? And even if myth could be said to be true, which of the thousands of myths that exist or have existed is the correct one? Or can more than one myth be true? What is the nature of such truth?

## The Truth of Myth in General

First of all, it should be noted that the terms true and false have not been found in all societies. The preliterate societies in which this was the case did, nevertheless, make distinctions among the stories they told, some being regarded as "not serious" while others were held to be "serious." Perhaps these terms are precursors of "false" and "true," which are found among virtually all literate societies.

The terms true and false are widely used in the life-world. Gossip, stories in tabloids about politicians' private lives, and statements of fact arising in the commerce of daily life, whether private or public, may be said to be true or false. Since it is in the life-world that I have situated myth, it may be expected that its truth or falsity will be found there. On the other hand, given the nature of myth as orienting persons for living in the life-world, the question of at least a culture's own myth is rarely raised. Its truth, in an informal sense of the term, is held to be true implicitly.

Even when the terms true and false are used, their meaning varies from culture to culture. The Hebrew "*emeth*," for example, means "integrity," "firmness," and "solidity." These words might be used to characterize a piece of furniture which is well made, as if truth, like a chair, can bear up under a load without falling apart. There is a tactile quality to the word. Perhaps more importantly, however, "*emeth*" means "faithfulness." Here truth is an activity, a kind of temporality, a continuity with the past when facing the future. Faithfulness is not to be understood as Greek imitation; faithfulness is not replicating an eternal form. It allows for surprise, innovation, discontinuity. There is always the possibility that in the light of future events the continuity will be seen to be otherwise than at present. Faithfulness has to do with intention and is illustrated by Yahweh's ceaseless, difficult, and evolving covenantal relation to Israel.

"*Alétheia,*" the Greek term for truth, means "unconcealed-ness" or "uncoveredness." Its largely visual connotation is obvious. An examination of other cultures would discover still other meanings of "truth."

When philosophers or theologians raise the question of the truth of myth, however, they are not asking about its meaning in the life-world. They are not asking how engaged, committed people in a particular society regard their myth but whether that myth or even any myth may be validly regarded as true from a disinterested and universal perspective. "Truth" has been relocated from the life-world to the world of theoretical reflection.

This relocation itself, however, raises some red flags. "*Theoria,*" associated with terms for vision, derives from Greece. Moreover, the very idea of a theory of truth, which implies a rational conceptualization intuited by an intellect detached from and hovering over the material world, is, at least in the West, a child of the Greeks. Beyond that, if theories are reflections upon, thematizations of, and formalizations of meanings already having been generated in the life-world, then it would seem that the question of the theoretical truth of myth comes down to how Greek thinkers of a certain period in history and their contemporary progeny assess the stories they and others tell.

Such conclusions, of course, are too negative and too simple. Theories of truth do not seek to give direct expression to particular cultural biases but to take the measure of truth claims in the light of certain objective criteria. These criteria are often discussed in the context of the philosophy of science. The empirical or correspondence criterion, for example, states that among rival theories purporting to explain a phenomenon the one that is best supported by or most completely corresponding to the data, evidence, or experience is the one that is true or to be preferred. The coherence criterion states that the theory whose concepts are most free of logical contradictions and possessed of the greatest number of internal connections among concepts is the one that is true. The criterion of comprehensiveness states that the theory which accounts for more of the available data or facts is the true one. The aesthetic criterion states that the theory which is simplest, most elegant, or most beautiful is true. The aesthetic criteria are applied to the highly mathematical conceptualizations of theoretical physics. The fruitfulness criterion states that the theory which generates the greatest number of testable hypotheses or which in a variety of other ways is most productive is the true one. Finally, the pragmatic criterion says that theory is true which "works" best in certain specified (usually nonintellectual) ways.

By now, however, I hope that the reader, having become sensitized by this work to look in unaccustomed places for clues to the presence of myth, is feeling uneasy for the reason that the criteria themselves appear to be myth-dependent. The correspondence theory, which asks about the relation of an idea to the reality it represents, owes much to the Craftsman of the Timaeus, who is completely outside both the forms and the copies made of them and can, therefore, observe how well the latter match the former. In its empirical form, the criterion owes something to Genesis with its implications that this world is real, good, and knowable in a finite way by the senses. The coherence theory, emphasizing the presence of logical interconnections and the absence of contradictions among concepts, is based upon a consideration of the relations among Plato's forms and, therefore, is rooted in the Timaeus, as is the aesthetic criterion with its links to beauty and mathematics. Comprehensiveness is possible only from the alleged eternal and transcendent perspective created by Greek thinkers. As for the pragmatic criterion, historically the least influential of the lot, I would be delighted (perhaps on the aesthetic grounds of neatness or symmetry) to be able to demonstrate its relation to the story of the founding of Rome, the least highly regarded root of Western culture. The improvised rearing of Romulus and Remus by a mother wolf is certainly a pragmatic rather than an ideal upbringing. The emphasis the story places on the animal "origins" of the brothers implies a pragmatic mode of knowing that is far removed from the theoretical contemplations of a pure intellect which descended from a transcendent world above or which contains a spark of divinity.

The foregoing reflections imply that theories and criteria of truth are already and necessarily myth-dependent and are, therefore, both ill-suited and inappropriate as criteria for appraising myth. Rather than theories or criteria judging myth, myths help generate and lend credibility to theories and criteria. If myth is not a theory but a form of language, apprehension, and intention linking background and foreground, the tacit and explicit, and orienting people for all activities, including the activity of reflection, even the activity of creating and applying theories of truth, then to mistake myth for theory and to test it by techniques or criteria designed for testing theories can only ensure that myth will be discredited. Also, to evaluate the myth of one culture in terms of criteria of truth rooted in a different culture is likely to produce the same result. In our hybrid culture in the West, that, indeed, has happened. Whenever disputes cannot be settled at more superficial levels of engagement, the disputants appeal to more fundamental principles. If this process continues, the succession of principles will lead finally to myth. In such situations myth is forced out of its proper domain in the background and pushed into a contested foreground.

The ultimate assessment of myth must be of a kind suited to the nature of myth as giving expression to apprehensions of the life-world and as functioning to provide an orientation for living in that world. Within those strictures myth is neither true nor false *in a theoretical sense* but viable or not viable for the tasks (both theoretical and otherwise) which confront us. This viability is not determined in intellectual terms but in the very process of living, by whether or not one is energized, whether or not problems are being solved, whether or not life is integrated at a variety of levels, whether or not it is endowed with a significance that pulls one toward the future in hope. Viability is not determined in advance of inhabiting a myth, and the continued viability of the myth is not normally under conscious review with the aid of explicit critieria, whether these criteria be idealistic or pragmatic in character. Viability is "assessed" in the course of tacit reliance upon clues which emerge from one's living in the world in accordance with the myth.

If, moreover, myth is rooted in the life-world, then, insofar as the patterns of the life-world are different for different societies, different activities will be selected as the preferred ones. Viability in any culture will be especially sensitive to those preferred or paradigmatic activities. If our Greek legacy urges upon us such activities as are associated with sculpture, architecture, drama, science, and philosophy,[47] it is because those were preferred activities in its life-world, and the viability of the Timaeus as both expressing and supporting these activities is related to the viability of these activities as a special style of being-in-the-world. While there is, to be sure, some overlapping, the preferred activities lying behind Genesis are less technical, less narrowly vocational. Genesis recommends not certain specialized activities but a certain value-orientation in all activities. It supports the making of moral and existential choices, especially those fundamental choices bearing on the total trajectory of one's life as it moves toward the future in relation to neighbor, nation, and God.

Myth as such makes no philosophical or scientific or theological claim. Its intention, as we have seen, is different. It lays down a world in which theoretical enterprises subsequently become possible. In relation to theories myth pleads nolo contendre. It cannot, therefore, be judged directly or with certainty by theoretical reflection to be true or false. Myth, on the contrary, generates theories of truth and falsity and undergirds such judgments, giving them existential force.

To this point, some postmodernists might agree with much that has been said. Their lingering commitment to modernism, however, would prohibit them from accompanying me further. It does not follow from what has just been said about criteria of assessment that they ought to be discarded as useless. If such criteria, themselves already myth-dependent, lack ultimate efficacy in the search for truth, they may yet play a significant, penultimate role. Polanyi, you will recall, spoke of knowing as having a "from-to" structure. The discovery that the criteria are not absolute, guaranteeing universal and uniform truths (the "to" pole of the structure), does not condemn them to being partisan cheerleaders for the particularities and idiosyncrasies of the cultures in which they were born (the "from" pole of the structure). Either approach cuts the intention and tension linking the "from" with the "to": both approaches proceed on modernist assumptions. We are not confined to airtight, impermeable cultural ghettos. Just as roots disappear from sight beneath the ground, so our rootage in a cultural tradition shades off into the tacit and unspecifiable ground which runs under and leaks through the explicit fences we sometimes set up. At the other pole, if critieria are unable to sever themselves from their origins in particularity, they do permit us, to borrow a phrase from Merleau-Ponty, to "slacken the intentional threads" connecting us to our roots and gain some fresh perspective on our own ultimate commitments and those of others. That criteria are abstract in character is a function of their effort to strip away the merely parochial as they strain toward the universal. They are the distillation of a culture's accumulated wisdom and experience in the search for truth. They are the culture on tiptoe, surveying itself and the curious terrain beyond the ambiguous border.

Within a finite model of knowledge criteria can be understood by analogy to a Polanyian "maxim," which is defined as

> ... a partial formalization of a personal act, which is to be interpreted within the context of this personal act. . . . Maxims are rules, the correct application of which is part of the art they govern. . . . Maxims cannot be understood, still less applied by anyone not already possessing a good practical knowledge of the art. They derive their interest from our appreciation of the art and cannot themselves either replace or establish that appreciation.[48]

Just as the rules or maxims of grammar do not preexist, Timaeus-like, the language they seek to guide but are made possible by that language, so criteria of assessment are the maxims of truth grounded in the collective acts that define a cultural tradition. The transcendence they achieve is partial and ambiguous, the very marks of finitude.

But if myths make no judgments and, consequently, their truth or falsity cannot be evaluated directly by criteria of assessment, then is not the understanding of criteria as maxims futile? I do not think so. It may well be possible to approach the truth of myth *indirectly* insofar as one can use the criteria to assess the truth or falsity of the theoretical claims derived by the thematization of myth. This approach is somewhat analogous to the way in which scientists test theories indirectly by testing the verifiability or falsifiability of empirical predictions deduced from them. Approaching myth in this way will, of course, involve the same difficulties that plague the scientific approach. The scientific practice, for example, can yield no certainty because (among other reasons) it employs the invalid logic of affirming the consequent. Beyond that, there is the difficulty of which criteria to apply, how to apply them, and how to handle situations in which multiple criteria yield variant assessments. These applications are ultimately unformalizable operations; they are, as Polanyi indicates, part of the art they seek to govern. In the face of these obstacles one is, nevertheless, not reduced to silence.

How, then, might this approach work in practice—for example, in assessing the truth of the Timaeus and Genesis, especially where they lead to conflicting theoretical claims? This is a crucial question for Western civilization, whose intellectual dislocations stemming from modernist assumptions and the postmodernist critique of them, are, as I have indicated, understandable, in part, in terms of their reliance on one or the other of these myths. It is also crucial for a work such as this one, which has argued that a postcritical perspective must include an acknowledgment of one's reliance upon myth. It is made urgent, moreover, by the fact that while this work indisputably owes much to both the Timaeus and Genesis, it has, by virtue of adopting an existentialist-phenomenological framework for reflecting on myth, accorded a privileged status to Genesis. Clearly, a thoroughgoing attempt to undertake such an approach is beyond the scope of this work. I will limit myself, therefore, to the briefest of indications as to how it might proceed.

## The Truth of the Timaeus and Genesis

Let us assess the Timaeus and Genesis with the help of the empirical criterion as applied to the idea derived from it of knowledge as a construction. This idea, as we noted, is found in Kant as well as contemporary structuralist and poststructuralist thinkers. It amounts to a formalization of the Timaeus relocated in the human knower in accordance with the Cartesian "turn to the subject."

Imagine, first, the construction site for a new building. At one edge of the site will be stacks of lumber of various sizes, concrete blocks, bricks, perhaps decorative stone. Elsewhere on the site will be a temporary building in which are kept, among other things, a set of blueprints prepared by an architect. In addition, there will be carpenters, plumbers, electricians, stone masons, interior decorators, etc. These skilled laborers will construct the building by arranging the building materials, under the supervision of the contractor, in accordance with the blueprints. This shaping of discrete materials by an external agent in conformity to an ordering principle is what is normally taken to be the meaning of "construction."

Suppose, next, that you and I are in conversation about the sorry state of politics inside the Washington beltway. You say, "The Democrats have been in control of Congress for too long," to which I immediately reply, "The problem doesn't lie in Congress; it lies in the White House." Is my reply a construction? I certainly had no experience of visiting a mental storeroom (the memory?), inspecting the entire stock of words that constitutes my vocabulary, selecting the ones needed for a reply. Indeed, before the meaning was constructed (assuming, for the moment, it was), how could I have known exactly what words among the couple of thousand available to me would be appropriate? Nor did I have any experience of consulting a principle of organization, a formula, or a set of mental categories with which to direct the selecting or assembling of these words. In fact, I have no experience of myself as doing anything special except opening my mouth and speaking my reply as part of a continuing intention to communicate with you and to counter your Republican "bias."

Perhaps, then, it is in writing that construction occurs. Let us focus on the first sentence of the preceding paragraph, "Suppose you and I are in conversation about the sorry state of politics inside the Washington beltway," to see if it is a construction. Once it is down on paper or on my computer screen, I can reflect on it and decide that the Washington beltway is too remote an example and replace it with a local or state illustration. Perhaps politics is too upsetting a field and should be replaced by athletics. Maybe "sorry" is not sufficiently sophisticated or precise a word and a substitution is in order. My putting one word after another or moving them around on the page or screen, then, seems to bear some analogy to construction.

This impression, however, is a superficial one. At best it describes the mechanics of displaying the spatial embodiments of meanings on a flat surface and not the creation of meaning. No more than in the case of speech did I inspect and select words to be written or consult a rule or principle of organization except as these words and/or these rules were themselves an upsurge of meaning. Words appeared at the tip of my pen or on the surface of the screen as my fingers moved over the keyboard and as I strained to summon (from where?) a reply whose intelligibility both you and I could recognize.

Being a constructivist of a Kantian, structuralist, or poststructuralist persuasion, you may retort, "You may have no conscious experience of a construction, but one must have taken place above, below, or behind conscious thought." "What evidence can you offer for such a claim," I reply. "None," you admit. "Then you cannot appeal to the empirical criterion to support the claim," I respond.

As Jean-Francois Lyotard notes, "It doesn't seem discourse is able to tolerate for long the fact that something inarticulate and intractable remains beyond its grip."[49] The tacit or inarticulate is not taken as a marker of human limitation but is, for one habituated to modernist assumptions of omniscience, a flimsy veil which postpones but for an instant transparent vision. Hence, after but a moment you press the matter further. "But some such constructive operation is required for a rational, explicit explanation of your speaking and writing," you insist, shifting to the coherence criterion. "You are assuming then, that a fully rational, explicit explanation is possible," I counter. "Moreover, you seem to assume also that you, the subject who constructs, are somehow separated from the reality upon which the constructed meanings are imposed," I continue; "Indeed, if the construction model is to fit, you must exist outside of the words (the matter) which you are to shape." "That the appearance of meaning requires an insertion, an inner connection by means of a body, in a natural, social, and linguistic world, an insertion your theory cannot acknowledge, despite the fact that these features of the world undeniably and powerfully impress themselves on us and that they are the inescapable reality we unproblematically and authentically live everyday, indeed the very touchstone of what counts as reality, leaves you with an even more paralyzing incoherence," I conclude.

"Beyond that," I say, taking the initiative and moving to the comprehensiveness criterion, "insofar as constructivist theories have difficulty making room for the reality of time, the reality of matter (including bodies), and the validity of experience (including our experience of persons), and especially the experience of the tacit, the ambiguous, the not-fully-formed, indeed the whole of the life-world as something preconscious and indeterminate, then it does not measure up well to Genesis-based theories, which, not being burdened by the necessity to attain certainty or absolute clarity, can be nondualistic and more inclusive."

These reflections do not amount to an attempt to exorcise and eliminate the Timaeus. That would be neither possible nor desirable. In very simple terms the relationship between Genesis and the Timaeus is analogous to the relation between the concrete and the abstract: the former includes the latter, much as the specialized life-world of the Academy is contained within and parasitically dependent upon the Athenian polis, of which it is a part and from which it is separated by a temporary and permeable partition. This abstract-concrete relationship is already implied in a peculiar logical feature of story and narrative—namely, their ability to incorporate without distortion all the other literate forms, including mathematical formulas. Lacking verb tenses, proper names, and personal pronouns, none of the latter can, on the other hand, include stories without serious loss of meaning.

The abstractness of the Timaeus is also evident by the fact that nobody can completely live the Timaeus alone. To do so would be, to use Socrates' words, to "practice dying"—that is, the deliberate self-extrication from this world. Thus, the philosopher who gives a lecture based on modernist or ultramodernist assumptions promptly leaves them behind as he or she exits the lecture hall, making the well-practiced crossing from the specialized, partitioned professional world to the wider, richer, and more concrete life-world of which the former is a part.

The same relation obtains between the intellectual progeny of the two myths—namely, the various competing theories discussed in Chapter 4. That relationship is described more precisely by Merleau-Ponty:

> The relation of reason to fact, or eternity to time, like that of reflection to the unreflective, of thought to language or of thought to perception is this two-way relationship that phenomenology has called *Fundierung*: the founding term, or originator—time, the unreflective, the fact, language, perception—is primary in the sense that the originated is presented as a determinate or explicit form of the originator, which prevents the latter from reabsorbing the former, and yet the originator is not primary in the empiricist sense and the originated is not simply derived, since it is through the originated that the originator is made manifest.[50]

His statement in the Preface that phenomenology is a philosophy "which puts essences back into existence" is, in my terms, an effort to reintegrate the Timaeus into Genesis. That task requires the recognition that,

> the world is always 'already there' before reflection begins—as an inalienable presence; and all its efforts are concentrated upon re-achieving a direct and primitive contact with the world, and endowing that contact with a philosophical status.[51]

Merleau-Ponty's aim to give philosophical status to the life-world is a convergence with an insight of Polanyi's:

> We must now recognize belief once more as the source of all knowledge. Tacit assent and intellectual passions, the sharing of an idiom and of a cultural heritage, affiliation to a like-minded

community: such are the impulses which shape our vision of the
nature of things on which we rely for our mastery of things. No
intelligence, however critical or original can operate outside
such a fiduciary framework . . . the whole system of acceptances
that are logically prior to any particular assertion of our own,
prior to the holding of any particular piece of knowledge. . . . I
believe that the function of philosophic reflection consists in
bringing to light, and affirming as my own, the beliefs implied in
such of my thoughts and practices as I believe to be valid; that I
must aim at discovering what I truly believe in and at formulating the convictions I find myself holding . . . [52]

This does not, as it may appear to from modernist assumptions,
amount to confession in the sense of "a soliloquy by an individual
through which is revealed his merely personal and idiosyncratic
uniqueness" but, as William Poteat explains, the recovery of "an
ancient, pre-Cartesian model—Augustine's *Confessions*" in which
what is confessed is

both *given* and *shared*. This recovery of the prepersonal and
personal historical roots of one's own knowledge leads, not, as
for the Cartesian, to subjectivism or relativism, but to the recognition of the inescapable, because necessary, universal intent of
all our affirmation.[53]

What Polanyi terms "our vision of the nature of things" and "the
whole system of acceptances" includes myth—namely, that original laying down and taking up of a home in a prereflective world
of meaning-being.

This does not mean that one cannot be open to dialogue with
others of a different point of view. It does mean that reaching
agreement as a result of persuasion becomes less probable the less
the two discussants inhabit a shared world. Even so, given that the
roots of our knowledge are largely tacit and unspecifiable, it is
impossible to map the boundaries of one's openness. Moreover, as
the Zen monk who suddenly and unexpectedly achieves satori
upon hearing the sound of a rake striking gravel might say, it is also
impossible to predict what piece of evidence, bit of logic, line of
argument, use of imagery, tone of voice, gesture of body, personal
joy or tragedy may overturn the conviction of a day or a lifetime.

Perhaps a confession of Gandhi best articulates this ambigu-
ously open, finite, from-to (*from* given and shared world *to* uni-
versally intended truth) structure of knowing:

I simply want to tell the story of my numerous experiments with truth, ... as my life consists of nothing but those experiments. ...

What I want to achieve—what I have been striving and pining to achieve these thirty years—is self-realization, to see God face to face, to attain *Moksha*. ... All that I do by way of speaking and writing and all my ventures in the political field, are directed to this same end. ... Far be it from me to claim any degree of perfection for these experiments. I claim for them nothing more than does a scientist who, though he conducts his experiments with the utmost accuracy, forethought and minuteness, never claims any finality about his conclusions, but keeps an open mind regarding them. ... One claim I do indeed make and it is this: *for me they appear to be absolutely correct, and seem for the time being to be final. For if* they were not, I should base no action on them. But at every step I have carried out the process of acceptance or rejection and acted accordingly. And so long as my acts satisfy my reason and my heart, I must firmly adhere to my original conclusions.[54] (emphasis mine)

# CHAPTER 6

# *Epilogue*

In the previous chapters I have examined the fortunes of myth in relation to modernity and then sought to set forth a new understanding of myth from a postcritical perspective. In the pages that remain I wish to reconsider modernity in the light of the imagination, connect the modern imagination to the life-world of the ancient Greeks, and comment briefly on the New Guinea story with which this book began. Finally, I intend to recommend an epistemological allegory appropriate to a world now leaving modernity in its wake.

## THE VISUAL IMAGINATION

Early in Chapter 2 I adopted Susanne Langer's view that, philosophically speaking, modernity can be defined in terms of the bifurcation of reality into inner experience and outer world. This ontological dualism, along with the epistemological dualism based upon it and the critical rhetoric stemming from it, are largely a matter of theoretical judgment. Modernity, however, is not merely a matter of doctrine. It is also a matter of imagination. The transformation of imagination which led to modernity consisted in the reorganization of our sensibilities in the direction of what Walter Ong has called "visualism,"[1] an arrangement of priorities among the senses in favor of visual perception. Ultimately, it led to the fashioning of intellectual standards and a technico-critical rhetoric based on the characteristic qualities of vision. In the West the language in which acceptable discourse of a serious kind must be articulated has, as a consequence, a decidedly visual bias.

Like the activities of the intellect, the operations of the imagination are rooted in the life-world. Visualism in the West is rooted in the life-world of ancient Greece. That life-world was not purely subjective but reflected an ongoing encounter with an inherent feature of the natural environment. I refer to the light whose peculiar qualities, known to artists even today, permeated the Hellenic scene. The effects of that light are noted by C. M. Bowra.

> What matters above all is the quality of the light. . . . The beauty of the Greek landscape depends primarily on the light, and this has had a powerful influence on the Greek vision of the world. Just because by its very strength and sharpness the light forbids the shifting, melting, diaphanous effects which give so delicate a charm to the French or the Italian scene, it stimulates a vision which belongs to the sculptor more than to the painter, which depends . . . on a clearness of outline and a sense of mass, of bodies emphatically placed in space, of strength and solidity behind natural curves and protuberances. Such a landscape and such a light impose their secret discipline on the eye, and make it see things in contour and relief rather than in mysterious perspective or in flat spatial relations. They explain why the Greeks produced great sculptors and architects, and why even in their painting the foundation of any design is the exact and confident line.[2]

The effect of this light was not to eliminate the significance of the other senses but to produce a sensorium especially sensitive to sight and perceptual habits reflecting its "logic."

The invention of alphabetic script reinforced the visualist sensorium, which soon manifested itself in a distinctive literary style. Erich Auerbach, who traces visualism (the tendency to eliminate background in favor of foreground) through the history of Western literature, explains the extended digressions, absence of suspense, and multitude of epithets in Homer's *Odyssey* in terms of

> . . . the basic impulse of Homeric style: to represent phenomena in a fully externalized form, visible and palpable in all their parts, and completely fixed in their spatial and temporal relations. Nor do psychological processes receive any other treatment: here too nothing must remain hidden and unexpressed. . . . Homer's personages vent their inmost hearts in speech; what they do not say to others, they speak in their own minds, so that the reader is informed of it . . . and no speech is so filled with anger or scorn that the particles which express logical and grammatical connections are lacking or out of place. . . . Never is there a form left fragmentary or half-illuminated, never a lacuna, never a gap, never a glimpse of unplumbed depths. . . .

The Homeric style knows only a foreground, only a uniformly illuminated, uniformly objective present.[3]

Auerbach contrasts the Homeric style with the Hebraic tendency, evident in the story of Abraham's sacrifice of Isaac, to minimize foreground in favor of background. In Ong's terms the Hebrew sensorium reflects an oral-aural configuration.

According to Bowra, the "secret discipline" of light imposed itself not only on the composition of epics and dramas but also played a role in the emergence of philosophy.

> Nor is it fanciful to think that the Greek light played a part in the formation of Greek thought. Just as the cloudy skies of northern Europe have nursed the huge, amorphous progeny of Norse mythology or German metaphysics, so the Greek light surely influenced the clear-cut perceptions of Greek philosophy. If the Greeks were the world's first true philosophers in that they formed a consistent and straightforward vocabulary for abstract ideas, it is largely because their minds, like their eyes, sought naturally what is lucid and well-defined. Their senses were kept lively by the force of the light, and when the senses are keenly at work, the mind follows no less keenly and seeks to put in order what they give it. Just as Plato, in his search for transcendental principles behind the mass of phenomena, tended to see them as individual objects and compared his central principle to the sun which illuminates all things in the visible world and reveals their shapes and colors, so no Greek philosophy is happy until it can pin down an idea with a limpid definition and make its outline firm and intelligible.[4]

These visualist perceptual and intellectual habits, then, constituted part of the life-world of both pre-Socratic and Socratic Greece.

If, as I have argued, myth is a comprehensive and originary attempt to articulate a culture's life-world for the purpose of getting a better grip on that world and living in it more effectively, then we should not be surprised to find that the Timaeus embodies and expresses so perfectly a visualist sensorium. By contrast to creation in the P-account of Genesis, where so much of significance occurs off-canvas and is ultimately obscure even to Yahweh, world origins in the Timaeus occur out in front of the reader and in full view. The Forms or Ideas possess the utter clarity of pure intelligibilities and each is thoroughly distinct not only from the others but also from prime matter and the Craftsman, whose constructive movements do not spring from hidden intentions but are governed essentially by the Forms. Nor should anyone be surprised that this visualist style of imagining and thinking should issue in a logic containing the principle of excluded middle, in which all the grays of thought and reality are banished forever in favor of pure and simplistic blacks and whites.

Modernity inherited and imparted a new intensity to this visualist style. In terms of the imagination modernity can be defined as that era in which the sensorium became not merely predominantly but almost exclusively visualist and the reduction of background to foreground became absolute. A number of factors contributed to this development. First, Gutenberg's printing press, as Ong observes, seemed to "lock" linguistic meaning ever more tightly and inescapably in space,[5] that identifying dimension given primarily to sight.

Second, the neo-Pythagorean revival, which began in Florence, intensified interest in mathematics, especially Euclidean geometry, that form of math whose spatial illustrations make it peculiarly accessible to visual perception. It was not an accident that Galileo, a Pythagorean, called sight "the most excellent of the senses."[6]

Third, for the handful of neo-Pythagorean scientists, Euclidean geometry described actual space; reality was characterized by Euclidean structures. For everyone else, Euclidean geometry constituted a merely mathematical space. Instrumental in closing this gap in favor of the Pythagoreans was the work of Renaissance painters who made use of the technique of linear perspective, an application to art of Euclidean geometry. Through their paintings Giotto, Masaccio, and others taught the populace to understand the world as Euclidean. They turned an abstract mathematics into a space in which people believed themselves to live and move and have their being.

Just as Descartes systematized and supplied a philosophical foundation for the new ontology generated by Kepler and Galileo, so he also consolidated and established as "normative" the intensified and exclusively visual imagination. For him, humans are endowed with the "natural light of Reason" which "illuminates" objects as do the "rays" of the "sun." Ignorance is "blindness," and the evil that must be overcome is "darkness" or "obscurity" or "vagueness." He refers to man as a "spectator" of the objects upon the earth and even records that for nine years he roamed the world "seeking to be a spectator rather than an actor in all life's dramas."[7] Moreover, in defining "reason" and "intuition," pivotal concepts in his epistemology, Descartes fell back on the language of light and sight. In a passage instructing the reader in the proper employment of the power of intuition, Descartes, who also wrote a book on optics, explicitly draws the analogy between the operation of the intuition and the eye:

> How the mind's intuiting powers may best be employed can be learned from the manner in which we use the eyes. For he who endeavors to view a multitude of objects all at once in a single glance sees none of them distinctly; and similarly anyone who is wont to attend to so many things at once in a single act of thought does so with a confused mind. But just as workmen who engage in tasks calling for delicate manipulation, and are thereby accustomed to direct their eyes attentively to single points, by practice acquire a capacity adequately to distinguish things which are subtly minute, so likewise with those inquirers who refuse to have their thought distracted. Occupying themselves with the things that are simplest and easiest, these too become perspicuous.[8]

When he insisted that clarity and distinctness, two patently visual concepts, were the criteria for determining truth, the form of the modern imagination was set.

The governance of our conceptual frameworks by visualist models is not without consequence, as Walter Ong has shown.[9] Sound, for example, places a person in the middle of an auditory world. It comes toward the ear not only from the front but also from below, above, and behind. Surrounded by sound, one feels almost inescapably a part of the sound-given world. Because sound is generated only when activity is taking place, this auditory world is active, energetic, and one is swept up in the activity, becoming a participant. Sound also opens up access to interiors. A violin string is plucked and discloses the structure of the cavity of the resonating chamber. Likewise, a body-subject speaks and, in so doing, discloses a person's feelings and thoughts.

Sight, by contrast, gives one access to only what is in front of the eyes. What is out of sight, says Ong, what cannot be made into a front, does not, in effect, exist. In that sense sight is inherently abstract. Sight also allows for a certain distance to develop between seer and seen. The seer can become a spectator rather than a participant. Sight plays over a space of moving or motionless material objects, and, insofar as it seeks clarity, examines the particulars of this visual space in a one-at-a-time sequence. Sight is the perceptual power ideally suited to dissection and thus promotes fragmentation and atomism. Finally, notes Ong, sight gives access to surfaces only. As light is reflected from surfaces, so vision's efforts to penetrate a surface and reach the interior are repelled.

The consequence of the foregoing, I contend, is that when sight became an imaginative paradigm for knowing in general, we were conditioned to think of the mind as an eye[10] gazing at a two-dimensional surface arrayed before it and knowledge became that fraction of reality that could be transmuted into images inscribable clearly and distinctly on that surface. To know became to emit a vacant, disinterested stare at the luminously displayed "forms." This visualist surface has been given a variety of names: "*tableau visuel*" by Merleau-Ponty, "presence" by postmodernists, "mirror" by Richard Rorty, and "blackboard of the mind" by Marjorie Grene. I find the last to be particularly appropriate by virtue of the fact that it is upon the blackboards of our elementary and secondary school classrooms that we are formally introduced to the plane figures of geometry and the numbers, diagrams, and formulas of arithmetic and algebra, those disciplines Descartes esteemed for their certainty.

If Descartes could so readily conclude that his true self had nothing whatsoever to do with his body, it was because as part of visualist space, conceived in terms of Euclidean primary qualities, the body was utterly hostile to any inherence of spirit. If spirit seemed to acquire in the modern era a more intensely individualistic, transcendent, and rationalistic character, it was the result of being radically deprived by visualist criteria of any material matrix. And if it is the very nature of myth to gather up comprehensively the life-world, which is the background of all backgrounds, and to articulate it in a condensed, ambiguous (from the point of view of modernist theories) narrative form, then myth can find no place on the visual blackboard and, therefore, no place in modernity. In terms of the imagination, modernity is the era of pure foreground.

In Chapter 1 we embarked upon a quest to identify the who, how, and why of the "murder" of a New Guinea tribe, on the suspicion that what happened to it in a matter of six months had been happening to Western civilization imperceptibly over the course of centuries. By now we should not be surprised that the immediate instruments of death in New Guinea were mirrors, photographs, movies, and (one may speculate) writing. Besides being fetishes of twentieth-century wizardry, they embody a total orientation to life which is hostile to myth. This orientation has as its end the elimination of a past which hindered the achievement of certainty. Doubtless, the longing for certainty at the outset of modernity was prompted by such factors as the disintegration of the medieval synthesis; the Protestant Reformation; the loss of the pope as a single, overriding, and unifying authority; and the onset of protracted religious wars.

Yet, like the narrator in William Golding's *Free Fall*, who set out to retrace the events of his life in order to isolate the moment when he had fallen into sin but found that no such clear moment existed, our quest, too, may have merely made things more complicated. Is the murderer Carpenter, the Australian government, Descartes, Galileo, Plato, or Pythagoras? Was the murder weapon a mirror, Kantian constructivism, visualism, geometry, the *Timaeus*? As for certainty as a motive, it surely moved Plato every bit as much as it did Descartes. Perhaps one of the major lessons of the recovery of myth and the whole prereflective world it embodies is the impossibility of finding neat answers to such simple questions. If so, how are we to think of the more complex era opening up to us as modernity fades?

## NAMING THE NOMAD

In the famous Greek mythlette Narcissus saw his reflection in the water and believed it to be another person. In the modern age we have done the reverse. We have looked at the visualist blackboard and seen the image of a mechanistic object, a ghostly spirit, a naked ape, a selfish gene, or a computer and believed them to be *ourselves*. What are the images that will characterize postmodernity? Several have already been suggested.

Mikhail Bakhtin has called the new age one of "carnival," which Nathan Scott interprets as a time

> . . . in which "life is drawn out of its *usual* rut" or is in some radical way "'turned inside out.'" That is to say, all the customary hierarchical structures and all the conventional norms and protocols are suspended, as the common life is invaded by a

great wave of riotous antinomianism that makes everywhere for
bizarre *mesalliances*. Things that are normally separate and distinct are brought together, so that "the sacred (combines) with
the profane, the lofty with the low, the great with the insignificant, the wise with the stupid." And the presiding spirit of blas-
phemy finds its quintessential expression. . . . In short, everything is topsy turvy, and the disarray engenders an uproarious
kind of laughter.[11]

In terms of interpreting texts Barthes sees it as a time for "erotic
play."[12] Epistemologically, Mark Taylor sees it as an age of
"erring."

Is there, however, any genuine joy in the play or fun at the carnival or delight in the laughter? If not, then perhaps the explanation for that is the one Morris Zapp gives to Fulvia Morgana in
David Lodge's novel *Small World*.

"And now Derrida," said Fulvia Morgana. "Everybody in
Chicago—I've just been to Chicago—was reading Derrida.
America is crazy about deconstruction. Why is that?"

"Well, I'm a bit of a deconstructionist myself. It's kind of
exciting—the last intellectual thrill left. Like sawing through the
branch you're standing on."

"Exactly! It is so narcissistic. So 'opeless."[13]

"Play" and "carnival" may well be a counsel of despair for those
who understand that modernity is hopeless and understand nothing more. The judgment of Terry Eagleton is that much of post-
structuralism is " . . . a hedonist withdrawal from history, a cult
of ambiguity or irresponsible anarchism. . . . "[14]

If the aim of much current criticism is simply to ensure and
revel in an unending stream of interpretation on the view that a
text has no referent, then at the least such thought is merely a kind
of instrumentalism—namely, a technique for keeping criticism
afloat. It is also mere aestheticism in the Kierkegaardian sense—
that is, governed by what is interesting rather than by a commitment to what one believes to be good, true, and beautiful.

As for "erring," it is no better a description of our situation
that was "certainty." Experience tells us that life is an ambiguous
mixture of succeeding and failing and that what appears at one
moment to be an error will often merit a different judgment on
another day, and vice versa.

Perhaps "carnival," "erotic play," and "erring" are but the latest revival of the orgiastic rites of Dionysius and the skepticism and relativism of the Sophists. They are the manifestations of a conditioned reflex already two millennia old—namely, to swing wildly from one cultural extreme to another, from Dionysian to Apollonian excess. Since Sophism and Dionysianism were among the forces against which Plato reacted in his creation of rationalism and a transcendent world in relation to which this earthly one became devalued, to reemphasize the former can only be expected to trigger a subsequent and more virulent reappearance of the latter.

Perhaps the more fundamental problem is not choosing between polarized Dionysian or Apollonian solutions but our habit of looking exclusively to Greece for guiding images. This reflex is ironic in view of the fact that many of the most outspoken critics of what I will call the Timaeus tradition are Jewish.[15] Among them are Jacques Derrida, Emmanuel Levinas, and Michael Polanyi. In addition to Dionysius, Mark Taylor does offer the image of the nomad.[16] While nomadic existence can connote Hebraic roots, Taylor does not make that connection. Indeed, the generalized "nomad" has some of the characteristics of a Platonic form. The nomad has neither name nor face.

I wish, therefore, to recommend Abraham as a guiding image for what I hope is the emerging postcritical era. In so doing, I am naming the nomad who, as part of the tradition inspired by Genesis, may well have already been a tacit influence in the critique of modernity. I would point, however, not to the story of Abraham's sacrifice of Isaac—a story overrated as a clue to faith and the religious life—but to the fact that he left Ur of the Chaldees, as St. Paul put it, "not knowing where he was going."[17] Despite the probable historicity of some elements of the story, I will call the Abraham story an "epistemological allegory."[18] Its epistemological features are homologous with the interpretation of the P-account of creation given in Chapter 4.

Abraham left Ur of the Chaldees without knowing his destination but not without a reason. He had been given the promise of a "land flowing with milk and honey" and of descendants as numberless as the grains of sand. Upon closer examination, however, the promise is incredibly vague. How many is numberless? Are these descendants to be understood in a biological sense, a racial or ethnic sense, a cultural sense, a political sense, a spiritual sense? And where is this land? Is it a physical place or a spiritual condition? If physical, then no actual place bearing that name or description existed. It was not, like an Easter egg, hidden in advance for Abraham to find. Furthermore, Yahweh gave him no map, no checklist, no definition, no explicit criteria, no photograph, no surveyor's coordinates by means of which to identify the place if he should happen upon it. In fact, Abraham never did reach the land which subsequent patriarchs and judges came to call the Promised Land. Reflecting upon this extraordinary state of affairs, one is led to the conclusion that Abraham will find it, if at all, only as he is transformed by the journey itself and only as he is able to create from some merely suitable place something more.

Yet Abraham does not quite fit the image of nomad which Taylor advocates, if by that term is meant one who wanders aimlessly or who mindlessly follows where the herds go or even one who merely searches for fresh pastures. To picture Abraham's movements as purely spontaneous suggests that he lives in a momentary present cut off from past and future. Abraham, by contrast, has dreams, intentions, ambitions that go beyond grazing. He is searching for something, the Promised Land, but does not quite know what or where it is. The direction he travels is shaped not only by present circumstances but also by past experience and by the approach of a future whose possible scenarios he continually sketches, modifies, and resketches. His trajectory is not a circle, a straight line, or a spiral; it is nothing that can be plotted in advance or which even in retrospect can be adequately expressed by any geometrical figure, regular or irregular.

He is confident some of the time that he is making progress, but is less than certain. Although he has no definitive proof that he is closer to the promised land today than he was a month ago, he is not without pertinent evidence. He can point to sunrises, sunsets, waterholes, mountain peaks and passes, and other features of the terrain as they are familiar, unfamiliar, or of doubtful familiarity. And he can point to the positions of stars. More importantly, however, he is grasped by a vision of a land of promise, and that vision is the framework in which features of the terrain or sky are able to become clues or evidence. However incomplete from an omniscient perspective his evidence may be, he is confident enough to press on.

The epistemological significance of this elaborated Abraham story is apparent when juxtaposed to the story of the slave boy in Plato's *Meno*. There, Menon poses a dilemma which highlights the difference between Genesis and the Timaeus, between classical

Greek and "classical" Hebraic ways of thinking. How can one go looking for something? For if one already knows it, there is no need to look for it. Or, if one does not know it, then, even if one stumbles upon it by accident, one will be unable to recognize it as that for which one is searching. This dilemma, which assumes the logic of excluded middle, asks one to choose, in effect, between the extremes (the polar opposites) of complete ignorance or complete knowledge. In a choice that is fateful for the Western intellectual tradition, Socrates picks complete knowledge (omniscience). The choice is, as he acknowledges, an act of faith (although this fact is quickly forgotten), which he justifies by saying that at least the assumption of knowledge, unlike the alternative, will promote continued seeking.

In the biblical story, by contrast, Abraham's search for the Promised Land is paradigmatic for an entirely different possibility precisely because his journey crosses the land between Menon's extremes. This land is not the Land of Ignorance, the Land of Knowledge, or the Land of Erring; it is the Land of Learning (that ambiguous mix of succeeding and failing, knowing and not knowing). That Abraham did not reach Joshua's Promised Land emphasizes the character of the former as a perpetual learner. His is what Gerhart and Russell would call "knowledge-in-process."[19] It suggests a finite model of knowledge. The meaning of "a finite model of knowledge" can be elaborated by comparing Derrida and Polanyi, two Jewish thinkers highly critical of modernity and the Western philosophical tradition.

Suppose we wish to define "justice." We might fall back on Plato and say, "Justice is giving a man his due." Definition occurs, then, when "justice" (the definiendum) is equated with or replaced by "giving a man his due" (the definiens). The meaning of "justice" is nailed down securely precisely insofar as the meaning of the words in the definiens is also nailed down. The latter requires, however, that "giving," "a," "man," "his," and "due", by turns, be defined. In other words, each of these terms must itself be replaced by still other words, whose definitions have yet to be supplied, and so on. The process will continue until one finds oneself reusing words whose definitions are indefinitely delayed. One is caught in a linguistic circle. Using a spatial metaphor, Derrida would say that the meaning of "justice" is "dispersed" or "disseminated." In temporal terms the meaning is "deferred"— that is, continually postponed. In the language of semiotics one might say that the signifier ("justice") has become disconnected from the signified (the meaning of "justice"). What is true of single words is all the more true of sentences or entire texts. Following this logic, one may well conclude—and Derrida's doctrine of "undecidability" seems so to conclude—that we do not know what we are talking or writing about.

The same approach is used to undermine binary oppositions, which are at the heart of Structuralism.[20] Take, for example, the constrasts I have made in this work between Greek thinking based on the Timaeus and Hebraic thinking based on Genesis. Derrida might say that whereas my representation of Greek thinking ought to concern itself with Greek thinking alone, in fact it departs from this purity of representation by making references, tacit or explicit, to Hebraic thinking. It sees Greek thinking not as it is in itself but only in those ways in which it is believed to differ from Hebraic thinking. My conceptualization of Greek thinking depends, in part, for its meaning, then, on my conceptualization of Hebraic thinking, and vice versa. The meaning of "Greek" or "Timaeus" has become disseminated by a "leakage" or "hemorrhaging" into the meaning of "Hebraic" or "Genesis."

Derrida, then, paints a picture of meaning absenting itself, or meaning flowing away, of meaning disintegrating, of meaning being dispersed and lost, leaving only absence, an emptiness of presence. Polanyi's "unspecifiability" is roughly analogous to Derrida's "undecidability." He means that the grounds, evidence, or justification for any knowledge claim—and that would include the interpretation of texts or the definition of a word—cannot be specified. Here Polanyi and Derrida converge.

Polanyi's claims, however, are carefully qualified. He says that the grounds of our knowledge claims are "not completely specifiable" or cannot be "exhaustively specified." This qualification is important; it makes clear that he is not simply rejecting presence and embracing absence.

Moreover, for Polanyi, an act of perception or knowing is a movement in the opposite direction from dissemination. It is a collecting, a gathering together, an integration of tacit clues in a vectorial from-to thrust toward a relatively more explicit foreground of meaning. Because the from-to, tacit-explicit, subsidiary-focal relation is constitutive of knowing/meaning for Polanyi, it is no more a matter of absolute presence than it is for Derrida. Neither is it, however, a matter of complete absence. Perhaps, then, the difference is merely one of emphasis; Derrida sees the cup half empty while for Polanyi, it is half full.

The difference, I believe, is more fundamental. Take the distinction I have drawn between Greek and Hebraic ways of thinking. Clearly it is not so simple a matter as a binary opposition. My interpretation of the P-account of creation in Genesis was explicitly contrasted with the Timaeus, to be sure, but also with the Modoc account of creation and with the J-account in Genesis. The matter is even more complex. My understanding of both Genesis and the Timaeus depends upon both similarities and differences, not only with each other but also with Mesopotamian, Roman, Hindu, Muslim, and other Native American myths. Beyond that, there is my knowledge of the Hebrew language, Mediterranean archaeology, and my knowledge of my own world, which has been confined largely to the American South, punctuated by brief trips to India, Guatemala, Costa Rica, and Egypt. These complexities and the indefinitely larger number of others, both unnamed and unnameable, function tacitly in my effort to understand Genesis and the Timaeus. The Greek-Hebrew differentiation is but the way in which we try to make a tacit understanding explicit in reflection.

Doubtless, Derrida would agree to the greater complexity of the so-called binary oppositions but would understand it as illustrating the many additional ways in which meaning as presence is dispersed and, therefore, corrupted. For Polanyi, on the other hand, the complexity just makes available so many more "clues" to rely on, so many more helpful perspectives upon the object of focal attention. These clues are viewed positively as increasing the probability of a satisfactory knowledge of that phenomenon in much the same way that walking around a piece of sculpture to appreciate it from a variety of perspectives provides a more adequate acquaintance with it and makes possible a better (but still incomplete) understanding of it. Even if my Greek-Hebrew contrast were a simple binary opposition, cognizance of that would likely be, for Polanyi, a reminder to be attentive and sensitive to the phenomenon under investigation rather than evidence of faulty description. Derrida is certainly right, over and against Structuralism, to reject binary opposition as an explicit and universal rule of interpretation. Yet, to borrow the language of Gestalt psychology, one phenomenon provides the "background" against which the "figure," constituted by the other opposition, becomes visible. Without some polarization of the perceptual field, nothing is perceived. According to a finite model of knowledge, reliance *at some point* and to some degree upon binary oppositions (including, for example, the finite-infinite opposition) may be understood as one of the conditions for there being any description at all. Indeed, reliance upon clues, both tacit and/or explicit, is a necessary condition for any act of perceiving or knowing by an incarnate, finite perceiver or knower. Only an omniscient deity needs no such reliances.

With respect to the attempt to define "justice" Derrida would be concerned to demonstrate the undecidability of meaning, how definition eludes us. Polanyi, by contrast, would be concerned to show how, despite the *ultimate* (according to an infinite model of knowledge) unspecifiability of the meaning of words, understanding and definition occur nonetheless (according to a finite model of knowledge).

What I detect here is not merely a matter of diverse emphases but of disparate models of knowledge. The embodiment of tacit clues is not, for Polanyi, a defect of knowledge; it is constitutive of it. It is the *conditio sine qua non* of there being any knowledge at all. It opens up the standpoint, the vantage point from which perceiving and reflecting can be launched. In other words, in his *Personal Knowledge: Towards a Post-Critical Philosophy* Polanyi is putting forward a finite model of knowledge. That all knowledge has a tacit component is the meaning of "postcritical." That tacit component, with all that it entails, is, in fact, the mark of finitude.

Derrida, on the other hand, despite the frequency and intensity of his attacks upon the tradition of Plato and Hegel, apparently remains captivated by the Western intellectual tradition in at least this one respect—namely, in the model of knowledge which is *tacitly at work in his rhetoric*. This insight is not altered by the fact that Plato and Hegel are said to be absolutists while some poststructuralists and Deconstructionists (ultramodernists) are said to be relativists, for absolutism and relativism are but two sides of the same coin. Epistemological absolutism says that knowledge, if we can have it, is omniscient in nature, and *we can have it*. Relativism says that knowledge, if we can have it, is omniscient by nature, but *we cannot have it*. The model of knowledge is the same; the difference lies only in the propects for fulfilling it.

Those who continue to embrace the omniscient model, even while they protest against it, are compelled to flee to the very kinds of binary opposites that Deconstruction wishes to under-cut—namely, from presence to absence, from author to no author, from foundationalism to groundlessness, from objectivity to subjectivity, from static structure to chaotic change.

I do not doubt that Derrida would deny that his epistemology is based on omniscience and that he has merely swung from one position to its binary opposite. He might even say that he and Polanyi are engaged in remarkably similar projects. He could even cite passages from his works to shore up these denials. My claim, however, is not about Derrida's explicitly held epistemology but the epistemology implied by his critical rhetoric. In other words, his *rhetoric* ("undecidability," for example) indicates that it is still more important to him to critique the past than to lay out a view which moves altogether beyond the options of the past. Even his more positive ideas, such as "text," "trace," and "writing," seem to be defined primarily by their distance from presence rather than by their distance from both presence and absence. In that sense at least, Derrida remains, however much on the periphery, within the gravitational pull of modernity and the Timaeus and unable to reach escape velocity.

Polanyi, on the other hand, does not entitle his major work *Personal Unknowledge* or *Personal Ignorance* but *Personal Knowledge*. Intentionally and more clearheadedly than Derrida, he has adopted a finite model of knowledge and made it the cornerstone of his epistemology. In so doing Polanyi directs his thought at right angles to both poles (absolutism-relativism, presence-absence) of the inherited intellectual tradition and, because substance and rhetoric are ultimately not separable, his is the more radical and more intelligible critique.

Polanyi's approach is consonant with Abraham's journey across the Land of Learning, a journey which takes us between the horns of Menon's dilemma. It delivers us from both the explicit absolutism and omniscience of the Western philosophical tradition (the "to" pole), on the one hand, and the skepticism and relativism (reverse or tacit absolutism) of much of Postmodernism (the "from" pole), on the other. The Abrahamic paradigm exhibits both the from-to structure of Polanyi and the *Fundierung* of Merleau-Ponty. Abraham, who lies within the orbit of Genesis, is paradigmatic for a finite model of knowledge.

# NOTES

## CHAPTER 1. MODERNITY AND THE CRISIS OF MYTH

1. Edmund Carpenter, "Television Meets the Stone Age," *TV Guide* 19, no. 3 (January 16–23, 1971), 14.
2. Ibid., 16.
3. Lévi-Strauss would be delighted by the scene in Brian Moore's book, *Black Robe: A Novel* (New York: Dutton, 1985), recently made into a movie, in which Father LaForgue, a Jesuit priest en route to a missionary outpost among the northern Iroquois, dramatically demonstrates to his native guardians/guides the power of writing. He asks their chief to tell him some personal secret. LaForgue writes the secret in a book and subsequently shows the page, in the presence of the chief, to another Frenchman. When the Frenchman reads aloud the written secret, the chief is amazed and frightened at the magical transmission. This leads the other guides to charge LaForgue with sorcery.
4. Philip Wheelwright, "Poetry, Myth, and Reality," in Gerald J. Goldberg and Nancy M. Goldberg, eds., *The Modern Critical Spectrum* (Englewood Cliffs, N.J.: Prentice-Hall, Inc., 1962), 319.
5. Richard Chase, *Quest for Myth* (Baton Rouge: Louisiana State University Press, 1949), chap. 1.
6. Edward Spicer, *Cycles of Conquest: The Impact of Spain, Mexico, & the United States on Indians of the Southwest, 1553–1960* (University of Arizona Press, 1962).

## CHAPTER 2. MODERNITY ON MYTH

1. Susanne Langer, *Philosophy in a New Key: A Study in the Symbolism of Reason, Rite, and Art* (New York: New American Library, 1948), 19.
2. Edwin A. Burtt, *The Metaphysical Foundations of Modern Science*, rev. ed. (Garden City, N.Y.: Doubleday and Company, Inc., 1932), 89.
3. René Descartes, a letter to Princess Elizabeth dated May 31,

1643, in Norman Kemp Smith, ed., *Descartes: Philosophical Writings* (New York: The Modern Library, 1958), 252.

4. Quoted in Richard Chase, *Quest for Myth* (Baton Rouge: Louisiana State University Press, 1949), 7.

5. For readers wishing a comprehensive survey, I recommend William Doty's impressive *Mythography: The Study of Myths and Rituals* (University of Alabama Press, 1986).

6. Chase, *Quest for Myth*, 47.

7. Bronislaw Malinowski, *Magic, Science and Religion* (Garden City, N.Y.: Doubleday and Company, Inc., 1954), 101.

8. C. S. Lewis, *God in the Dock: Essays on Theology and Ethics*, ed. Walter Hooper (Grand Rapids, Mich.: William B. Eerdmans Publishing Company, 1970), 66.

9. C. S. Lewis, *An Experiment in Criticism* (Cambridge: At the University Press, 1961), 43–44.

10. Lewis, *God in the Dock*, 66–67. For Descartes, God, like angels and human minds, lay on one side of a line separating thinking substances from extended substances. In classifying Lewis's theory as outside up I have drawn the ontological dividing lines to reflect recent views rather than those of Descartes.

11. Ibid.

12. Ernst Cassirer, *Language and Myth*, trans. Susanne K. Langer (New York: Dover Publications, Inc., 1953), 8.

13. Ibid., 99.

14. C. G. Jung, *Psyche and Symbol: A Selection from the Writings of C. G. Jung*, ed. Violet S. de Laszlo (Garden City, N.Y.: Doubleday and Company, Inc.), 87ff.

15. Robert A. Johnson, *He: Understanding Masculine Psychology* (Harper and Row, 1973), 31.

16. Joseph Campbell, "Mythological Themes in Creative Literature and Art," in Joseph Campbell, ed., *Myths, Dreams, and Religion* (New York: E. P. Dutton and Co, Inc., 1970), 168.

17. Ira Progoff, "Waking Dream and Living Myth" in Campbell, ed., *Myth, Dreams, and Religion*, 184.

18. Claude Lévi-Strauss, *Myth and Meaning* (New York: Shocken, 1979), 6–7.

19. The idea of myth as polyfunctional is not new. Joseph Campbell long advocated a view of myth as having cosmological, sociological, and metaphysical functions. These were subordinate to, if not quite reduced to, the psychological function.

20. Doty, *Mythography: The Study of Myths and Rituals*, 11.

21. Ibid., 10–11.

22. Ibid., 15.

23. Ibid., 7.

24. Ibid.
25. Ibid.

## CHAPTER 3. MYTH AT THE MARGINS OF MODERNITY

1. Arthur W. H. Adkins notes that Protagoras regarded both *muthos* and *logos* as legitimate modes of truth and that in Plato's dialogue of that name Protagoras is depicted as using both. This appears, however, to be an exception or a short-lived practice. See Arthur W. H. Adkins, "Myth, Philosophy, and Religion in Ancient Greece," in Frank Reynolds and David Tracy, eds., *Myth and Philosophy* (Albany: State University of New York Press, 1990), 105.

2. Mircea Eliade, *Myths, Dreams and Mysteries* (New York: Harper and Row, 1960), 25.

3. Mircea Eliade, *Myth and Reality* (New York: Harper and Row, 1963), 5–8.

4. Taylor Stevenson, *History as Myth: The Import for Contemporary Theology* (New York: The Seabury Press, 1969), 17.

5. Michael Novak, *Ascent of the Mountain, Flight of the Dove; An Invitation to Religious Studies* (New York: Harper and Row Publishers, 1971), 138–140.

6. Ibid., 140.

7. Eliade, *Myths, Dreams and Mysteries*, 24.

8. Harvey Cox, *The Secular City: Secularization and Urbanization in Theological Perspective* (New York: The Macmillan Company, 1965), 21–24.

9. Stephen Toulmin, "Contemporary Scientific Mythology," in Stephen Toulmin, Ronald Hepburn, and Alasdair MacIntyre, *Metaphysical Beliefs; Three Essays by Stephen Toulmin, Ronald W. Hepburn and Alasdair MacIntyre*, 2d ed. (London: S. C. M. Press, 1970).

10. Michael Foster, "The Christian Doctrine of Creation and the Rise of Modern Natural Science," in *Creation: The Impact of an Idea*, eds. Daniel O'Connor and Francis Oakley (New York: Charles Scribner's Sons, 1969), 39.

11. Langdon Gilkey, *Religion and the Scientific Future: Reflections on Myth, Science, and Theology* (New York: Harper and Row Publishers, 1970), 66.

12. Quoted from the *New York Times*. See Ibid., 80.

13. Edward Maziarz, "Science and Myths as Symbolic Structures" in George F. McLean, ed., *Myth and Philosophy*, Volume XLV of Proceedings of the American Catholic Philosophical Association, 1971, 61.

14. I refer to Ian Barbour's *Myths, Models and Paradigms: A Comparative Study in Science and Religion* (New York: Harper and Row

Publishers, 1974) and Mary Gerhart and Allan Russell, *Metaphoric Process: The Creation of Scientific and Religious Understanding* (Fort Worth: Texas Christian University Press, 1984). Barbour compares models (systematically developed metaphors) and paradigms (historical exemplars) in both science and religion. He regards myths as narrative analogies having a variety of functions, one of which is cosmological. Although he says that myths are often the source of religious models and theories, he makes no such claim for contemporary science. Ancient cosmologies, which would have come from root metaphors embedded in myth, he seems to regard as religious rather than scientific. The primary aim of Gerhart and Russell is to set forth a theory of "knowing in process." They quibble with MacCormac and Barbour over the precise nature of metaphor but follow MacCormac in saying that myth is the false attribution of truth to a scientific theory.

15. Earl R. MacCormac, *Metaphor and Myth in Science and Religion* (Durham, N.C.: Duke University Press, 1976).


## CHAPTER 4. MYTH IN THE HEART OF MODERNITY

1. Lawrence J. Hatab, *Myth and Philosophy: A Contest of Truths* (LaSalle, Ill.: Open Court, 1990).
2. Daniel O'Connor and Francis Oakley, eds., *Creation: The Impact of an Idea* (New York: Charles Scribner's Sons, 1969).
3. Stephen Daniel, *Myth and Modern Philosophy* (Philadelphia: Temple University Press, 1990).
4. Hereafter I will use *"Timaeus"* to refer to the written work and "Timaeus" or "the Timaeus" to refer to the story of origins contained therein.
5. José Ortega y Gasset, *The Modern Theme*, trans. James Cleugh (New York: Harper and Row Publishers, 1961), 53–55.
6. Alice Marriott and Carol Rachlin, *American Indian Mythology* (New York: New American Library, 1968), 45.
7. Claude Lévi-Strauss, "On Bricolage," in *The Savage Mind* (London: Weidenfeld and Nicolson, 1966).
8. Thus Alan Watts' charge that creation in Genesis is "fluky" would be more appropriately directed toward the Modoc story. See Alan Watts, "Western Mythology: Its Dissolution and Transformation" in Joseph Campbell, ed., *Myths, Dreams, and Religion* (New York: E. P. Dutton and Co., Inc.), 19.
9. That there are in Genesis no preexistent and eternal forms is obvious enough. My interpretation here, which is indebted to Michael Foster, does require an ex nihilo view of matter. Since creation out of nothing has been the dominant interpretation of Genesis in the Western

tradition, it is essential to follow that interpretation when arguing about the actual impact of the myth. See Michael Foster, "The Christian Doctrine of Creation and the Rise of Modern Natural Science," in *Creation the Impact of an Idea*, eds. Daniel O'Connor and Francis Oakley.

10. John Priest, "Myth and Dream in Hebrew Scripture," in Joseph Campbell, ed., *Myths, Dreams and Religion* (New York: E. P. Dutton and Co., Inc., 1970), 55.

11. John Macmurray, "The Hebrew Consciousness," in *The Clue to History* (New York: Harper and Brothers Publishers, 1939).

12. George Gamow, quoted in Frederick Hoyle, *The Intelligent Universe* (New York: Holt, Rinehart and Winston, 1983), 172.

13. Frederick Hoyle, *The Nature of the Universe* (New York: Harper and Brothers, 1950), 125.

14. Ibid., 123–24.

15. Stephen Hawking, *A Brief History of Time from the Big Bang to Black Holes* (New York: Bantam Books, 1988), 50.

16. Hoyle, *The Intelligent Universe* , 237–38.

17. See, for example, Gerardus van der Leeuw, *Religion in Essence and Manifestation: A Study in Phenomenology* (Gloucester, Mass.: Peter Smith, 1967 reprint of 1963).

18. See, for example, Joachim Wach and Joseph Kitegawa, eds., *The History of Religions: Essays on the Problem of Understanding* (Chicago: University of Chicago Press, 1967).

19. See, for example, Ninian Smart, *Worldviews: Crosscultural Explorations of Human Beliefs* (New York: Charles Scribner's Sons, 1983), 15–17.

20. Carl G. Hempel and Paul Oppenheim, "Studies in the Logic of Explanation," *Philosophy of Science* 15 (April 1948), 135–75.

21. Throughout this discussion I have been heavily indebted to Edward St. Clair, *Explanation in Science and Religion*, a doctoral diss. for Duke University (Ann Arbor, Michigan: University Microfilms, 1971), chap. 1.

22. C. G. Hempel, "The Function of General Laws in History," *Journal of Philosophy* 39 (1942). The issue is discussed in Ian Barbour, *Issues in Science and Religion* (Englewood Cliffs, N.J.: Prentice-Hall, 1966), 194–202.

23. William Dray, *Laws and Explanation in History* (London: Oxford University Press, 1957).

24. Arthur Danto, *Analytical Philosophy of History* (Cambridge: Cambridge University Press, 1965) and W.B. Gallie, *Philosophy and the Historical Understanding* (London: Chatto and Windus, 1964).

25. Roland Barthes, "Myth Today" in *Mythologies* (New York: The Noonday Press, 1972), 109.

26. Aristotle is often characterized as an empiricist. From the nar-

row perspective of Socratic philosophy and by contrast with Plato this characterization makes some sense. In the longer sweep of history, however, I tend to see the difference between them as slight. Aristotle rejected the separate existence of forms but retained the notion that form is intellectually distinguishable from matter. His "empirical" references, unlike those in modern empiricism, function as illustrations rather than evidence.

27. Michael Polanyi, "The Logic of Tacit Inference." *Philosophy* XLI (October 1966), 369–86. Polanyi's epistemology is most fully developed in his *Personal Knowledge: Towards a Post-Critical Philosophy* (New York: Harper and Row, 1958).

28. For a fuller discussion of this point see Thomas A. Langford and William H. Poteat, eds., *Intellect and Hope: Essays in the Thought of Michael Polanyi*, published for the Lilly Endowment Research Program in Christianity and Politics (Durham, N.C.: Duke University Press, 1968), appendix.

29. Polanyi, *Personal Knowledge: Towards a Post-Critical Philosophy*, 60.

30. Mary Hesse, quoted in Ian Barbour, *Myths, Models and Paradigms* (New York: Harper and Row Publishers, 1974), 33.

31. Ibid., 33–34.

32. José Ortega y Gasset, *Concord and Liberty* (New York: W. W. Norton and Company, Inc., 1946), 176.

33. William C. Placher, *A History of Christian Theology: An Introduction* (Philadelphia: The Westminster Press, 1983), 150.

34. Francis Oakley, "Christian Theology and the Newtonian Science," in *Creation: the Impact of an Idea*, 62–63. Oakley goes on to say: "Subsequent theologians had to do their thinking in the full glare of this persuasive clarification, and it is not surprising that many of them tended to set God over against the world which he had created, and to regard the order of this world as deriving, not from the realization of the divine ideas, but rather from the peremptory mandate of an autonomous divine will. This reaction was already manifest in the primacy over the divine intellect which Duns Scotus (ca. 1270–1308) accorded to the divine will, and it attained full stature in the ethical voluntarism of William of Ockham." Oakley also notes Pierre Duhem's recognition of the importance of 1277 for the natural sciences. See footnote on 83.

## CHAPTER 5. TOWARD A POSTCRITICAL UNDERSTANDING OF MYTH

1. Paul Davies, *God and the New Physics* (New York: Simon and Shuster, 1983), vii.

;leton, *Literary Theory: An Introduction* (Minneapo-
/innesota Press, 1983), 144.

'od and the New Physics, 107.

arbour, *Issues in Science and Religion* (Englewood
:e-Hall, Inc., 1966), 284ff.

ff.

kelstein, quoted in Gary Zukav, *The Dancing Wu Li
iew of the New Physics* (New York: Bantam Books,

piegelberg suggests the idea may have come to
>m William James rather than Brentano. See Herbert
ory of the Phenomenological Movement: A Histori-
ol. 1, 2d ed., (The Hague: Martinus Nijhof, 1971),

lerleau-Ponty, *Phenomenology of Perception*, trans.
n: Routledge and Kegan Paul, 1962), xi.
c.

iterary Theory: An Introduction, 146–47.
ussell Hanson, *Patterns of Discovery* (Cambridge:
ty Press, 1972), 23. A detailed comment on this
n chapter 2 of Mary Gerhart and Allan Russell,
*The Creation of Scientific and Religious Under-*
h: Texas Christian University Press, 1984).
anyi, "The Logic of Tacit Inference," *Philosophy*
369–86.
oteat, *Polanyian Meditations: In Search of a Post-*
m, N.C.: Duke University Press, 1985), 283–84.
*Time, Narrative, and History* (Bloomington: Indi-
1986).
d., 15.
d., 12.

itions, 163–64.
rary Theory: An Introduction, 145.
oteat, *A Philosophical Daybook: Post-Critical*
ia: University of Missouri Press, 1990), 10.
sworth, "Ode: Intimations of Immortality from
y Childhood" in *The Poetical Works of*
as Hutchinson (New York: Oxford University

26. Merleau-Ponty, *Phenomenology of Perception*, 90–95.

27. Michael Polanyi, *Personal Knowledge: Towards a Post-Critical Philosophy* (New York: Harper and Row, 1958), 64.

28. Sanford Krolick, *Recollective Resolve: A Phenomenological Understanding of Time and Myth* (Macon, Ga.: Mercer University Press, 1987).

29. Ibid., 34.

30. Ibid., 26.

31. Ibid., 41.

32. Ibid., 44.

33. Ibid., 57, 65.

34. Ibid., 74–75.

35. Ibid., 76.

36. Ibid., 84.

37. Ibid., 87.

38. See lines 327–64.

39. Psalm 8.

40. See Krolick, *Recollective Resolve*, 58–60, 99–102.

41. Ibid., 79.

42. William H. Poteat, "Myths, Stories, History, Eschatology and Action: Some Polanyian Meditations," in Thomas A. Langford and William H. Poteat, eds., *Intellect and Hope: Essays in the Thought of Michael Polanyi*, Published for the Lilly Endowment Research Program in Christianity and Politics (Durham: Duke University Press, 1968), 218, 226. Poteat's intention is to show how "action," "person," and "stories" function in different ways in the two types of myth and have their modern meaning only in eschatological myth. He explains: "Myths, in this classical sense, look very like stories and histories because the notation in which they are presented has tense distinctions, and because something seems to *happen* in them—in our sense of 'happen'. But in fact they are at least as much like what is given in tenseless mathematical notations, since what is given in them is eternal, or given eternally" (p. 222).

43. Cited in Mircea Eliade, *Myth and Reality* (New York: Harper and Row Publishers, 1963), 7.

44. Krolick, *Recollective Resolve*, 99–102.

45. Locke's sense data are modeled after Newton's atoms, which were, in turn, inspired by those of Democritus.

46. Tom Kasulis, "Kukai (774–835): Philosophizing in the Archaic," in Frank E. Reynolds and David Tracy, eds., *Myth and Philosophy* (Albany: State University of New York Press, 1990), 132.

47. Since philosophy is a form of reflection, it may seem inappropriate to mention it in connection with a life-world. Indeed, philosophy has depicted itself as having transcended engaged, committed, unreflec-

tive life. My point is that even philosophic reflection takes place in a context, a context which is taken for granted and tacitly relied on in innumerable and unspecifiable ways for the conduct of philosophic discourse. In the case of Plato, for example, that context would be the Academy, which itself is part of the larger context of Athens, Greece, and the world beyond.

48. Polanyi, *Personal Knowledge*, 30–31.

49. Jean-Francois Lyotard, "The inarticulate or the differend itself," a lecture delivered at Emory University, October 24, 1991.

50. Merleau-Ponty, *Phenomenology of Perception*, 394.

51. Ibid., vii.

52. Polanyi, *Personal Knowledge*, 266–67.

53. Poteat, *Intellect*, 18.

54. Mohandas K. Gandhi, *Gandhi: An Autobiography: The Story of My Experiments with Truth*, trans. from the Gujarati by Mahadev Desai (London: Phoenix Press, 1949), xi–xiii.

## CHAPTER 6. EPILOGUE

1. Walter Ong, *The Presence of the Word: Some Prolegomena for Cultural and Religious History* (New Haven: Yale University Press, 1967), 8–11.

2. C. M. Bowra, *The Greek Experience* (New York: New American Library, 1957), 23–24.

3. Erich Auerbach, "Odysseus' Scar," in *Mimesis: The Representation of Reality in Western Literature* (Princeton, N.J.: Princeton University Press, 1953), 4–5.

4. Bowra, *The Greek Experience*, 24.

5. Ong, *Presence*, 8.

6. Quoted in E. A. Burtt, *The Metaphysical Foundations of Modern Physical Science*, rev. ed. (Garden City, N.Y.: Doubleday and Company, Inc., 1932), 90.

7. René Descartes, *Discourse on Method* in *Descartes Philosophical Writings*, sel. and trans. Norman Kemp Smith (New York: The Modern Library, 1958), 115.

8. René Descartes, *Rules for the Direction of the Mind* in *Descartes Philosophical Writings*, 39.

9. Ong, *Presence*, 111–38.

10. William H. Poteat has shrewdly observed that what sees is *simply an eye*, without a body from which the eye is oriented. This follows from the fact that the lived body, the phenomenological body, does not belong to *res extensa*—that is, it is not describable in lengths, widths, breadths, and shapes. This insight is found in his unpublished manu-

script, "Persons and Places," 6. St. Paul, however, was probably the first to note the absurdity in the arrogation to itself of rule over the body by one of its parts when he wrote: "If the whole body were an eye, where would be the hearing? If the whole body were an ear, where would be the sense of smell? But as it is, God arranged the organs in the body, each one of them, as he chose. If all were a single organ, where would the body be?" See I Corinthians 12: 17–19.

11. Nathan A. Scott, Jr., "The House of Intellect in an Age of Carnival," in Donald W. Musser and Joseph L. Price, eds., *The Whirlwind in Culture, Frontiers in Theology* (Bloomington, Ind.: Meyer, Stone, and Co., Inc., 1988), 42.

12. Terry Eagleton, *Literary Theory: An Introduction* (Minneapolis: University of Minnesota Press, 1983), 142. He is describing the view of Roland Barthes.

13. David Lodge, *Small World: An Academic Romance* (New York: Macmillan Publishing Company, 1984), 118.

14. Eagleton, *Literary Theory: An Introduction*, 150.

15. Christopher Norris comments on the Jewish connection. See Norris, *Derrida* (Cambridge, Mass.: Harvard University Press, 1987), 228–29.

16. Mark Taylor, *Erring* (Chicago and London: The University of Chicago Press, 1984), 13.

17. Taylor Scott uses Abraham and Odysseus to contrast time in Hebraic and Hellenic culture. The journey of Odysseus from Ithaka to Troy and back forms a circle, while Abraham leaves Ur and never returns. See Taylor Scott, "Odysseus, Aeneas, and Abraham: Three Archetypes of Personal Identity in the West" (unpublished doctoral diss., Duke University, 1971). Sanford Krolick recommends Odysseus as a figure to symbolize his idea of mythic existence. See Krolick, *Recollective Resolve: A Phenomenological Understanding of Time and Myth* (Macon, Ga.: Mercer University Press, 1987), 93.

18. In using the term allegory, I do not mean to imply that there is a one-to-one correspondence between elements in the story and an act of knowing, nor do I suggest that the story was self-consciously told or written as symbolic.

19. Gerhart and Russell, *Metaphoric Process: The Creation of Scientific and Religious Understanding* (Fort Worth: Texas Christian University Press, 1984), 192.

20. Derrida's tactics here are quite similar to the *prasanga* method utilized by Nagarjuna, the founder of the Madhyamika School of Buddhist philosophy, in his attempt to blur the absolute distinctions at the foundation of the Abhidharma philosophy.

# INDEX